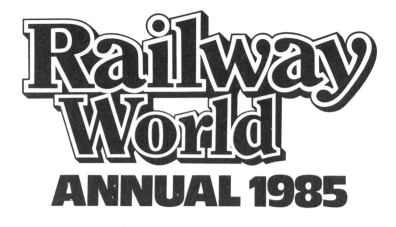

Railway World
ANNUAL 1985

£4.95

Cover:
'Castle' 4-6-0 No 5051 *Drysllwyn Castle* **at Nantyderry with the 'Welsh Marches Pullman' of 16 April 1983.**
J. H. Cooper-Smith

Previous page:
Was it really so long ago? The southbound 'Silver Jubilee', the 15.00 to King's Cross, waits at Edinburgh Waverley in 1977 behind now-preserved Class 55 Co-Co No 55.022 *Royal Scots Grey.* *G.S. Cutts*

This page:
A vigorous start from BR 2-10-0 No 92220 *Evening Star* **as it stomps out of Leeds station with the 'Bishop Treacy' charter train from the West Riding to Appleby on 30 September 1978. This took enthusiasts to the memorial service for Eric Treacy at Appleby.**
Brian Morrison

Overleaf:
Nicely caught atmosphere at Ellesmere Port No 2 box on 20 July 1983 as Class 40 1Co-Co1 No 40.172 sets out with the Ellesmere Port-Amlwch chemical tank train.

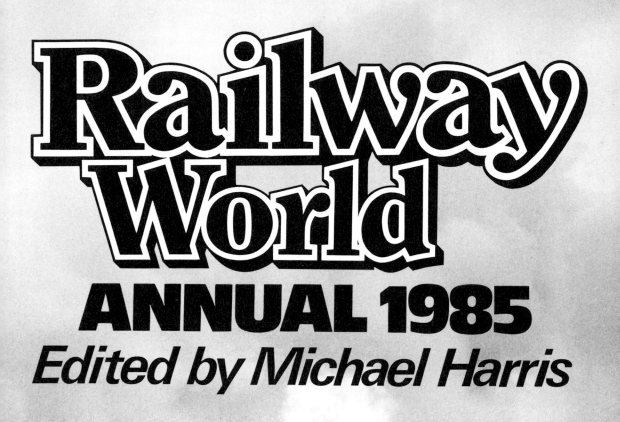

Railway World
ANNUAL 1985
Edited by Michael Harris

LONDON
IAN ALLAN LTD

First published 1984

ISBN 0 7110 1399 3

Published by Ian Allan Ltd, Shepperton, Surrey and printed by Ian Allan Printing Ltd at their works at Coombelands in Runnymede, England.

Contents

Overnight with 6S96 – the 'Soup Train'

Michael Harris

WHEN, from May 1983, the long-standing Harwich Parkeston Quay-Manchester Piccadilly boat train was extended to run to and from Glasgow and Edinburgh, mild interest was expressed in the way that the 'European', as it had been dubbed, would establish a link between the Continent, Harwich and Scotland. In fact, Railfreight, BR's sector name for its freight activities, had beaten the passenger people to it, and as far as Harwich and Parkeston are concerned, the list of inter-Regional Speedlink and Freightliner trains makes the 'European' look positively tame. The first air-braked wagonload inter-Regional service in East Anglia started in 1973, between Parkeston and Edinburgh, which by 1976 had become the 14.55 to Glasgow Sighthill. In addition, there was an Anglo-Scottish Freightliner train, the 19.45 Parkeston Container Terminal to Coatbridge Containerbase. Ten years after the start of that pioneer service, there are Speedlink trains from Parkeston to Paisley, Mossend, Warrington, Tees, Bescot, Widnes and Oxford, with return workings to Parkeston and Whitemoor, all but one

Below:
Class 08 diesel shunter No 08.752 shunts wagons for the Harwich train ferry in the down side yard at Parkeston Quay. *Brian Morrison*

conveying Continental traffic brought by the Zeebrugge-Harwich Town train ferry.

Freight traffic using the train ferry increased during the late 1970s/early 1980s but movement handling costs had moved out of line with receipts, so that drastic action was taken by BR's management in 1982 to get things back on the straight and narrow. That 'year of action' was also marked by the disastrous labour disputes between BR and the unions which naturally lost traffic to road, although most was recovered surprisingly soon.

The Harwich-Zeebrugge train ferry began after the Grouping, in April 1924, although the foundations for the service had been laid in Great Eastern Railway days. Before the introduction of cross-country Speedlink trains, the wagons moving from/to the train ferry were conveyed in Parkeston-Temple Mills/Whitemoor services, to be remarshalled into forward services from each of these yards. Nowadays, ferry wagons capable of less than 50 mph maximum speed are barred from BR's network; indeed 60 mph is the rule, but those capable of the lower limit are accepted by special arrangement. So the once-familiar pattern of the train ferry services has changed in a decade and,

provided costs can be contained, things look set for an encouraging future – modest though the ferry's capability seems alongside roll-on/roll-off trans-Continental road freight traffic.

Road traffic actually contributes to Speedlink's carryings. Anyone concerned at the volume of imported cars coming into the UK would not be reassured at the line-up of loaded car-carrying wagons waiting to leave Parkeston (or, indeed, Goole), and apart from the trainload services operated for distributors, cars also make an important contribution to Speedlink loadings. I was to see this during my overnight journey in mid-March 1983 on train No 6S96, the (then) 14.10 Parkeston Yard-Mossend Yard.

We arrived to find the train engine, 'English Electric' Class 37 Co-Co No 37.242, at the head of a 480-ton load: three loaded chemical tank wagons to Tyneside; three Cartic sets of imported Ford cars (two to Wakefield, one to Elderslie), and two vans for Ipswich.

No 37.242 looked smart externally, this Gateshead Class 37 having been outshopped by BREL Doncaster Works the previous month. It had received its last 'A' examination the day before my trip at Stratford Traction Maintenance Depot when it had been fuelled. At any rate, No 37.242 impressed the crew, Driver Shiel and Secondman Beech of Parkeston, who reckoned it 'a good 'un', pointing out that with a maximum permitted trailing load from Parkeston of 860 tons, No 37.242 wouldn't be overloaded on this occasion. The crew would work 6S96 to Whitemoor and return with the Manchester-Parkeston Quay boat train from March station. They were accompanied by Inspector Bell (London).

The last-minute discovery of defective brakes on two of the tank wagons delayed our departure, but with everyone eventually satisfied we left Parkeston 12 mins late on an overcast and breezy afternoon. The Harwich branch runs alongside the tranquil and attractive River Stour estuary to Manningtree, most of the climb at 1 in 117/134/154 to Wrabness being through woodlands. No 37.242 took 6S96 up the bank holding 45 mph, with 1,000 amps showing on the 'clock'. Driver Shell reckoned that a Class 37 'would pull anything up to 50 mph' but was liable to flag thereafter. The next station on the branch was Bradfield, closed to passengers in July 1956, but the station house remains. It is a curiously tall building with a steeply pitched roof and dormer windows and the driver amused me by saying that the station house was known to enginemen as 'Dracula's Castle'. Imagining the building silhouetted against a night sky, I could see what he meant! The schedule for 6S96 allows for a traffic stop at Mistley, which wasn't required today, and so we passed the station 5 mins early. The triangular junction at Manningtree was resignalled and rationalised in

Above:
Class 37 Co-Co No 37.242 stands in Ipswich Upper Yard with train No 6S96, on the occasion of the ride described in the article. Vans behind the locomotive, then the chemical tank wagons – and plenty of cars. Inspector Bell stands alongside the Class 37. 16 March 1983. *Michael Harris*

1980; we were checked before taking the now-singled curve from East to North Junctions. Having gained the main line, the train continued on the 'up road' until past the bridges at Cattawade, and once on the down line Driver Shiel opened up No 37.242 to climb up the 1 in 145 out of the Stour Valley at 35 mph, with 1,200 amps registering the energy expended in the process.

The 13.45 Norwich Liverpool St passed us not far off time before 6S96 topped the summit at Belstead, and now evidence of the forthcoming electrification was more marked, with lineside troughing for signal and telecommunications cabling, the renewal of a bridge arch for increased overhead clearances, and sight of a works train in the former Ipswich steam shed. After a check to a standstill at the north end of Ipswich station, 6S96 came to a stand in Ipswich Upper Yard still a few minutes to the good. Around us was evidence of a flourishing rail freight business, as diverse as a loaded bogie scrap wagon for Sheerness and a Freightliner train of Evergreen Line containers for Felixstowe. Ipswich sees a variety of traffic principally from Felixstowe and notably from the new Freightliner terminal due to open a couple of months after my ride on 6S96, but also from the town's own rail-served freight customers such as Norsk Hydro and the Docks. Ipswich was to give us a VGA (24.5-tonne capacity van) loaded with imported paper at Felixstowe and destined for Law Junction, and a Cartic set replete with showroom condition Volvo cars (loaded at Ipswich) for Wakefield. Our total train length was now 829 ft and the all-up weight, 528 tons.

Ipswich Upper Yard was busy with stabled Freightliner sets, so much so that an incoming Freightliner special from Temple Mills and headed by a pair of Class 37s was held fouling the main line.

Eventually it was accommodated and No 47.581 *Great Eastern* swept by with the 14.31 Norwich-Liverpool St; its first vehicle was Mk2D open first No E3170, renowned for its trip throughout by rail to an exhibition at Moscow in the summer of 1971.

6S96 set off from Ipswich 19 minutes early. Near Bramford we were slowed to 20 mph as a lorry had collided with a bridge parapet and remedial work was in progress; presumably the haulier involved escaped paying BR any recompense for what is an all too frequent hazard these days affecting railway structures. The cement works at Claydon with its prominent chimney is no friend to the environment and what was left of the locality's character has been destroyed by the new motorway standard A45 road towards Stowmarket. Before Needham Market on the up side is the Barham roadstone terminal, another example of the new rail freight traffic in East Anglia.

Approaching Haughley Junction, the wreckage could still be seen on the down side of the Norwich portion of the East Anglian TPO, the victim of a collision with another train in June 1982. But little remains of Haughley station, closed in 1967. At the time of my trip, the civil engineer had complete possession of the down Bury line whose alignment most nearly resembed the lowest grade freight railroad in the United States. The up road was being worked as a single line on tokenless block. We came to a stand east of Elmswell to allow the 14.53 Cambridge-Harwich Town diesel unit to clear. By now, it was raining and we passed Bury St Edmunds station, 26 miles from Ipswich, in 46½ minutes. Here, Class 45 No 45.016 was on hand, having run light after bringing in a block train to Kennett roadstone terminal.

Enginemen have traditionally identified lineside features which mark changes of gradient, and the summit of the Bury line at the now closed station of Saxham is indicated by a tree looking uncannily like a signal. Once over the top, 6S96 had no difficulty in running up to its maximum permitted speed of 60 mph, through this wide-open countryside with the characteristic lines of conifers along field edges. Soon we were in 'racehorse' country to the east of Newmarket, coming down to 25 mph for the Chippenham Junction-Snailwell Junction section; 6S96 had run the 9¼ miles from Saxham in 11 minutes. King's Snailwell scrapyard was the first doleful feature on what must be one of BR's less appealing sections of line – to Ely Dock Junction; certainly it looked bleak in the pouring rain of a March afternoon, at least until Ely Cathedral loomed out of the greyness. On the single line from Soham, worked on electric token, there was a permanent way slack to 20 mph for no less than 1½ miles; nonetheless we were still running to time.

Through Ely station, recovering after a check from a preceding Peterborough-bound diesel unit,

6S96 entered on another lesser known section of line, from Ely North Junction to March. Along here the climbs up to the bridges over the Wash and Sixteen Foot Drain are the most notable feature, the sections of level track marked by the characteristic ex-Great Eastern Railway gradient posts showing the symbol for infinity, rather than spelling out 'Level'. Between Black Bank and Manea, we passed a Class 31 at the head of the 16.42 Peterborough-Ipswich passenger train. Shortly afterwards, the crew pointed out a sizeable heronry occupying trees on each side of the line and I counted eight or so herons. West of Manea, a mile-long permanent way slack was imposed at the time in view of the poor condition of the track. Another deteriorating landmark on this line is Stonea signalbox which is shored up rather ominously but had survived like that for years, so I was told.

And now we were nearing March, heralded by a dismal collection of condemned diesel multiple-units en route for scrapping at Snailwell. Whitemoor Yard is now a pale shadow of itself, with neither hump yard operating, the Down Yard having completely closed during May 1982; since then traffic had been concentrated on the up side only on Roads 25-42.

Before November 1982, 6S96 had run on the Great Northern & Great Eastern Joint Line from Whitemoor to Lincoln and to Doncaster, but was then routed via Peterborough and the East Coast route, with the closure of the March-Spalding section.

6S96 is booked to spend 27 minutes in Whitemoor Up Yard, and the change of routeing to via Peterborough means that the locomotive must run round the train. The 15.10 King's Lynn-Whitemoor Class '7' feeder service brings traffic for 6S96, on this occasion one of the 15 curtain-sided PVB vans operated for Campbell's Soups consigned to a private freight depot at Law Junction and containing cans of soup for the Scottish market. This 'flow' of traffic is a clue to the title of the article! A barrier wagon was also added at what was now the rear of the train to protect the loaded tank wagons. From Whitemoor, Driver Wellings (Doncaster) took command and we also had the company of Inspector Geoff Mansell. Most Speedlink turns are single-manned, but there had been a two-man crew from Parkeston in view of 'Personal Needs Break' requirements of this turn.

The next section of our journey promised some excitement. We were booked down the East Coast main line soon after the main evening peak — how far would we be allowed to run on the fast road? We were away from Whitemoor 3 minutes late, and as 6S96 came underneath the East Coast main line at Peterborough, a Class 47 was bringing a down commuter train from King's Cross into the city. At the station the Harwich-bound boat train was waiting — our friends from Parkeston Quay could expect to be home on time, shortly after 21.00. The East Coast main line had not been free of problems on the day of my trip. Earlier on, Selby swing-bridge had been out of use and – unhappily coinciding with the evening rush – a door had been found open on a down Intercity 125 unit, so that the line had required searching as a result. At any rate, having been held in Peterborough station for 7½ minutes, once the 17.55 King's Cross-Bradford IC125 had belted through, 6S96 was allowed out on the down fast line.

Now that it was dark, the effect of the brilliantly-lit closed-circuit TV (or box) controlled level crossings was remarkable: their presence was obvious for several miles on straight sections of the line. Having worked up to 50 mph after Helpston, we were switched to the slow line at Tallington – eight miles start to pass from Peterborough in 14½ minutes. Shortly afterwards a down IC125 passed us. On the climb to Stoke Summit No. 37.242 kept the train rolling nicely with a steady 35/40 mph up the 1 in 178 beyond Corby Glen, so that the 23¾ miles from Peterborough had taken no more that 32½ minutes, and we were to pass Grantham on time. Behind 6S96 was the 18.04 King's Cross-York, but the operators obviously thought we would 'run' if given the chance. Their confidence in us was justified and we passed Tuxford, 55½ miles from Peterborough, in 62½ minutes, the sort of timing that would not have disgraced an East Coast express in steam days. From 60 mph on the level beyond the River Trent crossing north of Newark, No 37.242 held 45/50 mph on the 1 in 200 gradient past Egmanton — fair progress with our load. Indeed, 6S96 continued to have a clear run until Doncaster's suburbs came into view, but we encountered signal checks — and two signal stops — before coming to a stand ahead of the entrance to Belmont Yard, our next traffic stop.

The Class 37 now placed its train in the yard, a Class 08 taking over to remarshall 6S96 which typically sets out from Doncaster with five or six separate 'sections' of wagons to different destinations. Meanwhile, having been at the front end for over seven hours, a plateful of fish and chips and a mug of 'railway tea' were welcome fare to prepare us for the next leg of the journey to Tyne Yard, 109 miles away.

6S96 left Belmont yard with 17 loaded vehicles and two empties, a train weight of 566 tonnes. Apart from the soup, paper, cars and tank wagons gained earlier in our progress, Doncaster had contributed bricks from Butterley Bricks, near Newark; two vans loaded with glass bulbs from Harworth to Glengarnock; steel for Northern Ireland via Stranraer and BR spares. This train is booked for a crew change at Doncaster station, and on to No 37.242 came Driver Charles Foster (Tyne) and Inspector Peacock (York). The Class 37 had no difficulty working its train up to 60 mph before Selby, the view from the cab for several miles having been dominated to the left and right by the mega-power stations of Eggborough and Drax respectively. These days, the East Coast main line south of York is dominated by InterCity services. Gone are the days of the one-time crack Class '4' fitted freights, and Doncaster-New England, New England-Ferme Park Class '7' flows. With the closure of the March-Spalding section of the Joint Line and the diversion of Speedlink trains such as 6S96 to the main line, the picture has changed. Near Retford we had passed a Class 31 at the head of 6M66, the 21.21 Doncaster-Willesden Speedlink, running nearly 1¼ hours early, a Class 37 had brought a block oil train through Doncaster and an up Freightliner train was easing through Selby at the same time as 6S96. There was more activity at York Dringhouses, much of the locally generated traffic for Speedlink being the familiar confectionery brands made in the city. 6S96 took the goods lines through York to pass York Yard, now used only for recessing trains, where a train of imported Renault cars from Goole was waiting to follow us northwards. Our passing time at York Yard North

showed that 6S96 was 11 minutes early, having taken 45 minutes for the 33 miles from Doncaster station.

The next section was a delight as the Class 37 made light work of the easy gradients north to Northallerton along this 'racetrack' four-track main line. That said, the down slow line imparted some rough riding to No 37.242 until we were turned on to the down fast line at Huttons Wood, beyond Thirsk. On what was by now a clear, calm night there were at times three pairs of colour-light signals in our sights – each pair being about 650 yards apart. Beyond Northallerton we were passed by Speedlink 6E87, the 14.52 Mossend Parkeston, not far behind the last up day InterCity train, the 16.30 Aberdeen-York.

6S96 was still running early and, despite a permanent way slack to 10 mph beyond Croft Spa, the train passed Darlington South 12½ minutes early, having covered the 43 miles from York Yard North in 52½ minutes at an average speed of about 48 mph. Driver Foster gave No 37.242 'the gun' on the 1 in 220 up to Aycliffe, with 1,700 amps shown 'on the clock' and a minimum of 50 mph sustained to a healthy obbligato from the Class 37's twelve-cylinder 12CSVT prime mover. In the cab, we were eagerly waiting to see what Control would do with 6S96 so as to give precedence to the late-running 19.30 King's Cross-Newcastle InterCity 125. In the event, the signalman judged things well, turning us to the slow line at Ferryhill. Just as Driver Foster was preparing to slow the train to a stand, we were given the 'feathers' back on to the fast line before Tursdale. The rest of the run to Tyne Yard was easy and 6S96 came to a halt at 23.37, still eight minutes 'to the good'.

At the time, 6S96 was booked to pick up traffic at Tyne from 6S71, the 18.21 Whitemoor-Millerhill-Mossend and the latter arrived 5 minutes late at 00.40 behind Class 47 No 47.240 with Carlisle traffic to transfer to our load. Meanwhile, 6S96 was also awaiting a section of Renault cars from Goole for Stranraer off 6N64, the Hull-Tyne Speedlink 'feeder'.

Tyne Yard, although greatly reduced in extent since its short-lived heyday in the 1960s, is still an interesting place when it comes to train movements. One of the yard's Class 08 shunting locomotives was soon at work remarshalling the respective sections off 6S96, 6S71 and 6N64 to form the northbound departures. The outcome for our train was that with all the traffic offering it would have been over-length for the next section of its run, with the result that the middle section (for Mossend) was knocked out and marshalled instead in 6S71. As the train planners sorted matters out, two Class 37s moved out at 00.53 with 4S86, the 19.23 Nottingham-Coatbridge Freightliner (via Berwick), followed by the late-running Hartlepool-Leith company train of tank wagons. Then, 6S71 left at 01.32, nearly half an hour early. The locomotive for 6S96 was Class 40 No 40.158 which had brought in Speedlink 6E86, the 19.20 Mossend-Parkeston, and it backed down on to 6S96 at 01.13, our departure being further delayed by discovery of a fault on one of the wagons.

The last sections of 6S96's journey were among the most interesting. No 40.158 pulled away 24½ minutes late, and there was a crescendo of sound bellowing from the turbo-blowers of the 16SVT engine as the Class 40 passed underneath the various bridges at the north end of the yard. The trailing load was now 23 vehicles, of 504 tons. For the 65¾ miles Tyne Yard-Carlisle Yard, 133 minutes were allowed. This early morning journey convinced me of the impracticality of Dr Beeching's intention that all Newcastle-Edinburgh traffic should be routed this way, in view of the line's far from easy gradients, particularly in the westbound direction, and several speed restrictions and level crossings. Compared with the colour light signalling that had guided us so clearly on the East Coast main line from Peterborough, the preponderance of semaphore signals beyond Blaydon provided another opportunity to marvel at the engineman's ability to sight oil-lit signals on a dark night out in the wilds. The civil engineer's activities on the up line between Prudhoe and Hexham resulted in a signal stop, followed by single-line working with a pilotman. As a result, 6S96 was now running late, and further delays ensued at Haydon Bridge and beyond Haltwhistle, not to speak of a stop at Rock Fell for the signalman to advise us that How Mill's down distant was 'out'. Consequently, we came to a halt in Carlisle Yard 19 minutes late.

The re-ordering of 6S96 at Carlisle had a somewhat comic outcome. Having 'lost' our Mossend section at Tyne Yard, No 40.158 was now left with just two wagons, the 'soup' and the 'paper' for the Isis-Link depot at Law Junction. Consequently, the train would now terminate short of its booked destination. To save the cost of trip working, and because the depot has no electrified access, 6S96 is diesel powered north of Carlisle, so that the train engine can shunt at Law Junction. Despite being recessed at Abington to give way to a down sleeping car train, the Class 40 brought the featherweight load to its destination over 1½ hours early, at 05.50. Fifteen hours of footplating had provided a lot of interest. Although in the 'book' 6S96 can't rival the 'European' for a name, to Carlisle's enginemen at least it is the 'Soup Train'. And on my journey the 'Soup' reached its destination before time – Speedlink's equivalent, perhaps, of the Gravy Train.

The writer would like to thank the British Railways Board and BR Eastern Region for facilities provided in connection with this article.

The versatile GWR '43xx' 2-6-0s
Photo feature

One of the notable British mixed traffic steam locomotive designs was produced by G. J. Churchward, Locomotive Superintendent of the Great Western Railway. The first, of what became a class of 342 engines, was No 4301. After the first 20 were built in 1911, their numbers were swelled by Nos 4300/21-99 to 1916, then Nos 5300-99, 6300-99 and 7300-19 before 1922, with the exception of Nos 6362-69, turned out in 1925 with Nos 7320/21. Finally, came an 'improved' version, Nos 9300-19 of 1932. These had side-window cabs, screw reverse, and outside steampipes. The locomotive was over 3 tons heavier, and so this variety was subject to 'Red' route restrictions; the other '43xx' were classified 'Blue'. To combat flange wear on severely curved routes, the weight distribution was altered on 65 of the class in the '43xx' and '53xx' series. These became '83xx' in 1928, but were converted to standard, 1944-48.

From 1936-39, 88 of the class were withdrawn and their wheels and motion incorporated in the new 'Grange' and 'Manor' 4-6-0s. All the '43xx' engines were intended to be converted, but the onset of World War 2 put paid to the plan. Otherwise, the versatile 2-6-0s remained largely unaltered until withdrawals started in earnest from 1948. Nonetheless, the '43xx' class lasted almost to the end of steam on the Western Region. From 1956-59, the 20 '93xx' engines were each reduced in weight to make them comply with 'Blue' route restrictions and were renumbered 7322-41. Two '43xx' have survived for preservation, and, as restored, No 5322 is seen on page 109.

Below:
The '43xx' 2-6-0s were popular with the operating people for passenger work on secondary routes. No 6311 crosses the embankment south of Barmouth Bridge with a train for Ruabon on 24 July 1956.
R.E. Vincent

Above left:
The first of the series built in 1913, No 4321, is seen in original condition with pre-World War 1 lined-out livery. These locomotives – and all subsequent '43xx' – had slightly longer frames. Note the copper-capped 'wide' chimney. From No 5370, a standard cast-iron chimney was fitted and gradually appeared on the earlier engines.   *BR*

Left:
Works photograph of No 9319, the last-built '93xx'. Note that the safety valve bonnet is painted.   *BR*

Above:
No 5350, as newly outshopped in the last years of the GWR, and as fitted with outside steam pipes.
P.L. Melvill

Below:
No 5380 on a southbound freight train at Hooton on the GW and LNW Joint Birkenhead Joint Line in the 1920s.   *LPC/Ian Allan Library*

Above left:
The '43xx' 2-6-0s were capable of a fair turn of speed and originally were used on a number of fast passenger turns. By the 1950s, they could be observed on secondary passenger trains, and, like No 6368 passing Lansdown Junction, Cheltenham in June 1960, were turned out for excursion trains.   *John C. Baker*

Above:
In BR days, the class were painted black until, in early May 1956, Nos 6372/85 received lined green livery to work a Royal Train from Taunton to Barnstaple. From that autumn, green paintwork became standard. Newly outshopped No 6372 stands at Swindon Works on 1 May 1956.   *Stanley R. Watts*

Left:
A typical duty for a '43xx': No 5330 pulls away from Newton Abbot station with a Plymouth Millbay–Paddington parcels train in 1958. Note the gas tank wagon for 'gassing' restaurant cars behind the engine.   *D.S. Fish*

Below:
The Taunton–Barnstaple line was largely worked by these 2-6-0s in its latter days. One of 35 built by Robert Stephenson & Co in 1921/22, No 7304 was photographed near Wiveliscombe with the 10.02am Barnstaple–Taunton on 28 August 1961. Southern Region stock was diagrammed for some workings on this route, hence the appearance of one of the early Bulleid corridor sets.   *Michael J. Fox*

'93xx' engines in original form, and as converted to 'Blue' restriction route availability:

Top:
No 7340 enters Oxford station with an up freight in June 1964. 'Castle' No 7026 Tenby Castle **is at the head of a Paddington–Worcester express.**
I.J. Hodson

Above:
Reading main line pilot No 9308 removes a 70ft 'Toplight' slip coach which had been slipped from the up 'Cornish Riviera' express on 4 July 1955
R.L. Evans

SPB – Railway publicity king

Bel Bailey

SPB was a set of initials once as well known as GWR, LNER and the rest. It was short for Stewart Petrie Brodie Mais, a famous journalist and broadcaster in the 1930s and 1940s. SPB was also the finest railway promotional man this country has yet seen.

It all began around 1930, the year that SPB Mais was made redundant from his job with the *Daily* *Telegraph*, due to a change of ownership of the newspaper.

Luckily, a new career had unfolded for Mais with an interesting offer from W.H. Fraser, the GWR's enterprising Publicity Agent. In 1928, SPB had been asked to revise the Company's guides to Devon and Cornwall, having previously produced a free booklet for the Southern Railway called *My* *Finest Holiday*. Always an uncomprising individualist, SPB stood out for a free hand in this task. He insisted on treating the holiday counties purely on their merits and *not* strictly from a railway angle. The GWR agreed to this approach, reasoning that if SPB popularised Devon and Cornwall, most people would use trains to get there anyway!

The two GWR guides, in a bright and well-produced format, sold over 100,000 copies in 1928-34, but the railway bought the copyright, SPB being paid not royalties but a lump sum at the rate of so many guineas per 1,000 words.

This GWR advertising success alerted the other railway companies to SPB's possibilities. Soon, the LMS commissioned him to write a brochure on North Wales and also the 'Royal Scot'. The LNER commissioned him to describe its 'Northern Belle' cruising train, but of all the 'Big Four', the Southern Railway showed the most imagination of all. Pink handbills were distributed in London, the very first of their kind to offer a guided ramble linked with a special excursion train. The bills read boldly:

SOUTHERN RAILWAY – A MOONLIGHT WALK OVER THE SOUTH DOWNS To Witness SUNRISE FROM CHANCTONBURY RING With Mr S.P.B. Mais (of Wireless Fame) On SATURDAY (NIGHT) 16 JULY 1932

A special supper and breakfast car train was offered with Steyning as the destination, out on the

Left:
S.P.B. Mais and family at *Toad Hall***, Shoreham, c1938.**

Saturday night from Victoria, departing at 12.10 am. The return third-class fare was 4/- (20p), with the return from Steyning on the Sunday morning at 7.20 am.

The Southern Railway expected about 40 hikers or ramblers to turn up at Victoria for this pioneering trip. In the event, before midnight on 16 July over 1,300 had assembled!

It was hard to tell whether the waiting SPB, 'highly paid' for these jaunts, as he admitted, or the SR was the most surprised. But the company reacted magnificently and put on four trains at very little notice, to cope with this vast crowd.

For this was the heyday of the train-using hiker, when the pop-song of the year was 'I'm happy when I'm hiking'. The SR intelligently anticipated a growing trend in leisure. SPB later recalled his embarrassment on this first trip. When all the passengers arrived on Chanctonbury the moon had long gone down, but at 4 am the sun had not yet risen! The vast crowd of hikers gazed at him in disappointment and it took all his considerable powers of persuasion to convince the multitide that it was all good fun. . .

The early morning was damp and chilly, but the 1,300 travellers were determined to enjoy their odd experience and so all was well! From then on, the SR decided that it was on to a good thing. Many more jaunts followed, thereafter more carefully planned than that first improvisation. Incidentally, the pioneer trip went askew as the return trains were from *Amberley*, not Steyning!

SPB thoroughly enjoyed mixing with all the people on the trains and acted as 'guide, philosopher and friend' – a role that suited him down to the ground. He would stroll through the train, giving out leaflets on routes and chatting and answering questions non-stop. Numbers on these subsequent excursions settled down to about 400 on average. Most were young people and in the years of the Depression many were unemployed Londoners, hungry for fresh air.

Southern Railway Rambles followed from SPB's pen, consisting of rambles accompanied by maps and sold at 6d (2½p) each. Then the SR published his *Walking At Weekends*, encouraging train-users to stay in the New Forest or on the Sussex or Kent coasts, and describing little-known walks. Later, SPB extended this theme to cover all main stopping places on the route taken by the 'Atlantic Coast Express'. No wonder his broadcasts earned him the name of Ambassador of the Countryside! His warm, welcoming voice was as popular over the air as his railway brochures were to travellers.

From 1920-40, SPB lived on Southern Railway territory, first at 38 Brunswick Square, Hove, Sussex, then at 'The Hall', Southwick Green, thereafter at 'Toad Hall', Shoreham, where he and his family were unfortunately bombed out.

A sturdy traveller all his days, Mais died at the age of 89, in 1975. His travel books are many, but most keenly sought after are his famous railway advertising guides. They bring with them the very whiff of steam and adventure. SPB had that rare gift of making a railway trip even to the Home Counties sound as exciting as one on the 'Orient Express'. British Rail could certainly use him today!

Below left:
Title page of *Glorious Devon*, **published by the Great Western Railway, 1929.**

Below right:
Spirit of the 1930s: brochure for the 'Northern Belle' cruise train of the LNER. SPB produced a tour guide for the 'Northern Belle'.

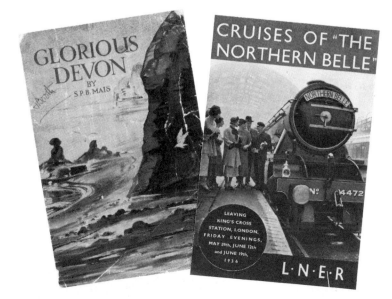

Encounters in Norway
Michael H. C. Baker

IN my article on foreign railways in the 1983 *Railway World Annual* I wrote about having a film confiscated by the Indian police. Not much fun, but in something close to wartime conditions it was perhaps not entirely unexpected. I also mentioned the delights of travelling through Scandinavian pine forests and of the 'Arctic Circle' express of the Norwegian State Railways.

Now, Norway is about as civilised a country as you could wish for, and it therefore came as a considerable shock to be told by a policeman in Steinkjer, about 80 miles north of Trondheim, that I was to accompany him to the station – and clearly he didn't mean the railway one. I'd been taking pictures at the railway station an hour earlier, but this after all was Norway so what had that to do with it? Perhaps I had illegally parked the car? I knew they'd got somewhat demanding about parking in the town lately. My sister who lives just outside Steinkjer – and with whom we were staying – had talked of an officious new warden. As I neither speak nor read Norwegian to any degree this explanation was possible.

But no. The policeman pointed to my camera lying on the seat beside me and, in excellent English, asked, 'Is that the camera you were taking pictures with near the station?' I said it was. Promptly, if carefully, he wound out the film. I was then invited, in the company of my nine-year old son and five-year old nephew, to accompany him. We must have looked a real bunch of desperadoes. Various personal details were copied down – my age seemed of particular concern – and then I was told to reappear the next day when the film would have been developed. More than this the Steinkjer police were not prepared to divulge.

When I returned to the house, my brother-in-law was hopping-mad. Having lived in many parts of the world, he rightly regarded his homeland as the land of the free and immediately rung up the police station. He was told that I had been seen on the wrong side of the tracks taking photographs with a

Below:
The 08.15 Trondheim–Bodo train, Norwegian State Railways, headed by Henschel/Brown Boveri Co-Co diesel electric No 4.654, built 1980.
Michael H.C. Baker

telescopic lens. This was true. In Norway, as elsewhere on the Continent, there are few fences and the local population tends to treat the railway as a public right of way. The low platforms and absence of footbridges and subways, other than at the largest stations, encourage such behaviour but I have never come across statistics suggesting that fatalities to unwary pedestrians are any greater proportionally than in Britain.

An hour later, the phone rang. My sister answered it, and turned to me with a grin, saying 'It's the press. They would like to interview you after you've been to the police station tomorrow. They think it will make a fine story.'

So lunchtime next day, my sister, her mother-in-law, and two eldest sons accompanied me into town. Once in the police station, my sister and I were shown to the office of the detective who dealt with aliens – I began to understand how immigrants at Heathrow must feel – and were ushered into a room with a Kandinsky reproduction on one wall and that of a half-baked looking, snivelling child on the other. I did not know what I was supposed to make of this. It was a very short interview. A quietly spoken man somewhat apologetically held up my film and said, yes, they had checked and I was an Englishman staying with my sister and her family in the district. The pictures were as I had said, of trains and I could take them back. My sister chatted briefly with the police officer in Norwegian, we shook hands and that was that.

There were sighs of relief all round on our reappearance and then we trotted over to the newspaper office, taking care to cross the railway yard by the subway rather than going across the tracks.

At the offices of *Tronder Avisa* I was met by Fiskum, the man who had telephoned the previous day. It was from him that I learned the full story.

He had seen the police car with its flashing light dashing down the main street, and, such being unusual in law-abiding Steinkjer, he had rung the police station to find out what was happening. He was given the facts and had then made some enquiries on his own behalf, checking with the NSB (Norwegian State Railways) area managers in Trondheim. Yes, he had been told, there *were* restrictions on taking pictures of railway installations, but no-one could recall them ever being enforced. It did seem as if the people at Steinkjer were over-reacting.

Apparently, photography of bridges is not permitted in Norway. If this law were ever enforced the tourist trade would take a nose-dive! Bridges are

some of the most spectacular and photogenic features of the country. Our approach by boat to Bergen from Newcastle was under a towering structure very like the Forth Road Bridge, and just about everyone of the 1,000 or so passengers on board the ferry was busily photographing the bridge.

Fiskum explained that railway enthusiasts were thin on the ground in Norway and the police and local railwaymen alike had found it hard to believe that there was not something sinister about a bearded character with a telephoto lens taking long and careful aims at various items of motive power, and then equally carefully going up to each subject and making copious notes. On top of this, the barracks were situated behind the station and directly in my line of fire.

It all began to make sense.

Readers will probably recall the many alleged sightings of Russian submarines in Norwegian fjords; the main E6 road which passes through Steinkjer continues, as does the railway line, to the Arctic Circle, and then to the USSR border. Once the police had checked that I had relations in Steinkjer and had written books and articles on travel and railways, then the temperature had dropped dramatically.

Right:
The writer at the 'scene of the crime' – Steinkjer station, Norway in 1983. *Tronder Avisa*

Above:
**Main line steam excursion in Norway: '21C' 2-6-0 No
225 and '24b' 2-8-0 No 236 head a fine set of typical
stock on a Vikersund–Krøderen working, 16 June
1983.**
John Scrace

Fiskum clearly thought the whole business was a
splendid joke, of which the police and the railways
officials were the butt. I thought this was a bit hard;
after all, strictly speaking I had been trespassing and
should perhaps have spoken to the station master
first. That said, I *had* sent a reply-paid request to the
NSB headquarters in Oslo before my visit and
received no answer.

The interview ended with all of us retracing our
steps to the station where Fiskum spoke to the
station master and we then took some officially
sanctioned photographs which Fiskum said he
hoped would make the back page of the newspaper
the next day.

Not a bit of it! Featured prominently on the front
of *Tronder Avisa* the next morning was a full-length
picture of me, complete with offending film and
camera, and standing in front of NSB locomotive
No 3.642. Beside the picture was the headline: 'I am
not a spy.' On an inside page were two more
pictures and six columns of text which included the
information that I had not brought my wife and
third son into town for the interview as I had heard
there was a law prohibiting more than six people in a
car and I didn't wish to be arrested two days
running! A slight case of rubbing salt in the wound.
The story was also broadcast three times that day on
Trondheim radio.

I suppose the moral is that one should not assume
one may take pictures of railway trains at will
anywhere in this world, but if the photographer is
going to get into trouble for so doing, then Norway
is a better choice than most.

As it happens, railway enthusiasts are not quite so
rare in Norway as I was to discover. Fiskum told me
of a preserved narrow gauge electric line south of
Trondheim, and while I didn't get to visit this I did
spend some time in the National Railway Museum
at Hamar where I had been four years previously.
This was followed by the highlight of my visit to
Scandinavia as far as the transport scene was
concerned – the sight of a delightful standard gauge

4-6-0 heaving a rake of beautiful, wooden-bodied
carriages up the side of a wooded valley north-west
of Oslo. There had also been a number of
developments on the main lines with some very
swish new carriages on the Trondheim - Oslo run,
bigger and better diesel and electric locomotives on
some of the principal passenger trains, and some
very smooth-running articulated trams in Oslo.

Norway tends to be remote from the mainstream
of European railways. In common with Ireland, it
had built its own rolling stock in the past, but has
increasingly imported equipment since World War
2. Some of its earlier locomotives came from
Britain; many new locomotives nowadays come
from Sweden and West Germany. The NSB may be
remote in one sense, but it is worth remembering
that the nearest railway station to the principal town
on the Shetland Islands is Bergen, and not
somewhere on BR.

Situated dramatically between the sea and the
mountains, Bergen is the most beautiful city in
Norway, and the construction of the 290-mile to
Oslo, the capital, was an enormous undertaking. It
was not opened until 1909, 55 years after the
beginning of railways in Norway, which gives some
indication of the work involved. One stretch is
above the tree line for over 60 miles, en route
passing through a bleak, glacier-strewn region from
where the snow never disappears, even in
midsummer. It seems extraordinary that for over 50
years the line was worked by steam and diesel
power, electrification not being completed until
1964.

Although modern locomotives and carriages are
to be found on the through trains, the electric

multiple-units which work between Bergen and Voss, 54 miles to the east high in the mountains, date back to the 1930s. Certainly, these sets look their age in their sombre rust-brown, unlined livery.

On the other hand, the magnificent new station at Oslo South, on which work was just beginning four years ago, is now in operation.

Although some of the old electric trains are to be seen there, there are also some brand-new ones numbered in the 69xxx series which tunnel under the city and emerge on the western side of the harbour. A few of the old wooden platforms exposed to the elements are still in operation at Oslo South. I couldn't see why expresses for Stockholm and Copenhagen had to use these when much of the new station was deserted, except during the rush-hour. Maybe it is sentiment. Outside the main cities, and even inside them occasionally, it is impossible to avoid forests for long, usually accompanied by mountains, lakes or fjords. But this is not surprising when one considers that only 8% of Norway is not so covered.

Norway is not immune from the recession which has hit the rest of the world, and unemployment is a worrying problem. But even though it no longer has a socialist government, Norway still has its priorities right and public investment remains at a high level. The observer can't help becoming cross when comparing the value most countries put on an up-to-date rail system, whether it is a sparsely populated one such as Norway, or one similar to ours such as France, against the miserly treatment that British Rail has suffered of late.

Just about the entire NSB system is worked by centralised traffic control and the only semaphore signals to be found nowadays are in the National Museum at Hamar. Electricity also powers something like 87% of all the NSB trains, although only 57% of the network is electrified. Electrification ends at Trondheim – only 18% of the population lives north of here, although the city is only one-third of the way up the coast from south to north. Part of the line from there, past sister Susie's, to the Arctic Circle terminus of Bodo has never seen anything but diesel traction, and the last section was not completed until 1962. Actually, it is not true to say that there is *no* electrification north of Trondheim. In 1901, a line was opened from the iron ore mines at Kiruna, in Sweden, to Narvik, a port on the west coast of Norway which is ice-free throughout the year, unlike the Baltic. Shortly

afterwards, Norway obtained its independence from Sweden. Today, the line is electrified, but it is still essentially part of the Swedish system, being independent from the rest of the NSB and worked by Swedish State Railways locomotives. Quite the most remarkable statistic concerning the Norweigian railways is that this mere 25 miles carries no less than *two-thirds* of all the freight passing over the NSB in any one year.

The red-brown livery adopted by NSB is not one of Europe's more imaginative, although splashes of yellow on the more recent rolling stock improves it a bit. Perhaps it evolved out of the varnished wood carriage and wagon bodies once universal. Steam locomotives were generally unlined black – typical Scandinavian abhorrence of shows of flamboyance.

The wooden carriages have nearly all gone from passenger service, although not from departmental use. Rather surprisingly, I came across one at Trondheim which had just worked in on the daily train from Stockholm, and a few appear on Oslo rush-hour services. A number are preserved. If the varnish is well-cared for, such carriages are a magnificent sight in the sunshine. The rake of vehicles, including two with clerestory roofs, which I saw in the charge of the 4-6-0 on the Kroderbanen looked splendid. This operation runs 16 miles from the Drammen – Honefoss line and is about 60 mins travelling north-west of Oslo. Equally fine were two such carriages at Hamar Museum. This also contained a remarkably luxurious compartment from a first-class coach built in Sweden around the turn of the century.

Although no longer involved with the construction of passenger rolling stock, the NSB probably makes more use of wood than any other railway system in the world. Almost all the catenary is supported by wooden poles, some of the early diesel shunters had wooden bodies, covered goods wagons are built of wood, and the type of vehicle which appealed to me perhaps more than any other in Norway was the goods brake van. Neatly labelled in raised metal characters 'Konductor', all were wooden-bodied, all ancient, and a number sported clerestory roofs. Norwegian wood is certainly far from dead!

Left:
Wooden-bodied clerestory buffet car at the NSB's Hamar Museum in August 1983.
Michael H.C. Baker

Below:
1927-built wooden goods brake van in a timber train at Valøy, August 1983. *Michael H.C. Baker*

Drivers wild

Derek Cross

I KNEW who it was as soon as I saw the Stranraer – Glasgow diesel multiple-unit come under the road bridge at the south end of Ayr station. It had the typical high-speed approach in the old Glasgow & South Western Railway tradition. There was a partial release of the vacuum brake, and then a full application. In those days, the station buffet at Ayr was opposite the exit to the platform and, as they had an early start from Stranraer, a cup of tea was called for, so the Stranraer men made sure that they stopped opposite the buffet. One man was a master of this art – Jimmy Irvine. I guessed he was the driver of the train that I was joining for my journey to Glasgow. One of the station inspectors at Ayr claimed that Jimmy was out of the cab of the diesel unit and on board again with his cup of tea before the train even stopped. This, I feel, must be ascribed to Ayrshire's notorious 'black' humour. 'Jimmy the Hare' they called him, not only because he was a grand runner – indeed, one of the best drivers I have ever had the pleasure of knowing – but because he had a hare-lip camouflaged by an Errol Flynn type of moustache. Jimmy was on the 'Paddy' from Stranraer–Ayr–Carlisle one evening during the last week of steam. The engine was 'Britannia' No 70038 *Robin Hood* and as they came into Ayr he spotted me on the platform and was off the footplate before the locomotive had stopped. 'Where are ye going, Derek?' he asked. 'London', I replied. 'Come on, then, it will be ye last chance of a ride on a steam locomotive to Dumfries.' As I was attending a meeting in London the next morning, for once I was dressed in a tidy suit and said that much as I would like to come it would not do my tailoring any good. Not to be put off, he told me to remove my jacket and, then, from somewhere or other, they found an old BR coat. With a final instruction to the sleeping-car attendant to: 'Hae a bucket o' hot water ready at Dumfries', I was bundled into the cab. The pilot engine was 'tied-off' at Ayr and we duly set out for the south by the Annbank line to Mauchline. Once past Blackhouse Junction, Ayr, Jimmy left his seat, handed me the regulator and, with the cryptic remark, 'Mind now, I never lose time on this job,' left me to get on with it.

I thought I was doing rather well as No 70038 was one of Kingmoor's better 'Britannias' until near Sanquhar I was informed, 'Ye're two (minutes) down so get a move on!' The curves of the Drumlanrig Gorge were not the best of places to be given this instruction, but it was a grand night and by the time we approached Dumfries the 'Paddy' was back on schedule. At the bridge over the River Nith, north of Dumfries, I reached for the brake to be asked abruptly, 'What the Hell do you think you're doing?' Rather naively I said, 'Well we *are* booked to stop at Dumfries'. 'Ye'll stop when I tell ye!' I then had a practical lesson as to why the G&SW section crews had the reputation of being

Below:
Driver Gordon Rennie (Ayr) awaits the 'off' when working 'Britannia' 4-6-2 No 70016 *Ariel* on the up 'Northern Irishman' Stranraer Harbour–Euston express on 22 February 1966. *Derek Cross*

Above right:
LMS '5' 4-6-0 No 44726 crosses Pinmore Viaduct on 23 February 1963 with a Stranraer–Glasgow train. This was after the great blizzard of that month which resulted in a ban on diesel railcars working south of Girvan. The driver is believed to be 'Booler' Marshall. *Derek Cross*

Right:
Barrhill on 18 February 1963. The morning Glasgow–Stranraer train departs behind Kingmoor LMS '5' 4-6-0 No 45126. This gives some idea of the vulnerability of the Girvan–Stranraer route to wind-driven snow. *Derek Cross*

such good brakesmen. We were still doing about 60 mph within a mile of the station when I was told to apply 'Partial release' – we were working vacuum. I did as I was instructed, but was conscious of the lights of the station coming up somewhat rapidly when Jimmy said: 'Right, give her the lot'. I did so with alacrity and we stopped. What is more, we stopped with the tender positioned right next to the water column. As we climbed out of the cab for the Carlisle men to take over, and Jimmy bade me good night he added: 'You know, given another 20 years of steam I could make a good driver out of ye yet'. This was the ultimate accolade coming from the late and much lamented Jimmy Irvine.

Over the years, a mystique has grown-up around some engine drivers, such as Bill Hoole, Bert Hooker and that most amusing man, Sammy Gingell, with whom I have had the pleasure of travelling on the footplate. I think I would be right in saying that this mystique probably began to develop during the 1888 and 1895 'Races to the North.' This was the first time in railway history that train working was closely observed by several eminent men who not only logged times and speeds but recorded the locomotive numbers, train loads and the enginemen's names as well. Between the world wars, this practice continued on the 'crack' trains recorded by the late Cecil. J. Allen, O.S. Nock, Kenneth Leech and many others, all of whom were punctilious when it came to noting the drivers' and firemens' names whenever they could. But they were generally observing the work of men in the top-links on well-known lines.

This essay is not concerned with such men, for two reasons: I have a bad memory for names and shall deal with locomen from one depot – Stranraer. Off the beaten track, it was little-known and, in steam days at least, best forgotten by the authorities. But Stranraer has had the reputation over the years of breeding generations of the 'Drivers Wild' of my title. This description is perhaps somewhat unfair, implying that they were reckless men. In most cases, this was untrue, but the routes to Stranraer from Ayr and Dumfries ran through wild country and the men who worked trains on these lines needed to have a ruthless streak in them. They had to be hard 'runners' and had to bend the rules. If they didn't there would have been no trains to Stranraer at all, especially during World

War 2 when the late-lamented 'Port Road' from Dumfries, and the even harder line from Ayr and Girvan over the bleak moors of the Chirmorie, were worked to capacity. Of the two lines to Stranraer, that from Girvan (or, for that matter, from Ayr) was the harder as it was built to a shoestring budget and had so many curves and changes of gradient that, in the days of unfitted goods trains, it was not just a case of hauling them *up* the hills, but keeping them in one piece on the way *down*. Coming to that, the art also lay in stopping them in the 'dips', too!

The 'Port Road', closed under the Beeching aegis, was the easier, even if the grades were longer for the most part. Also, it did not have the incessant curvature of the line to Girvan, although it saw heavier trains. When the 'Port Road' closed, the Stranraer-Girvan route had a weight of traffic thrust

Top:
Super-power for the morning Stranraer–Dumfries train on 22 May 1964, with LMS '5' 4-6-0 No 44957 leading BR '5' 4-6-0 No 73100 between Creetown and Gatehouse of Fleet. No 44957 has a Dumfries crew, No 73100 had Driver Willy Whannel at the regulator. *Derek Cross*

Above:
The thrice-weekly Whithorn branch goods leaves Whauphill on 26 April 1963, with Driver Jimmy Skimming in charge of Ivatt '2' 2-6-0 No 46467. Note the Pooley van (second in the train) for checking the weighbridge at Whithorn. *Derek Cross*

Above right:
'Give us a good start, Bob!' LMS '5' 4-6-0 No 45168 with Bob McCann makes a spirited re-start from Ayr No 2 signalbox with a Falkland Junction–Stranraer goods, having taken water. Photographer W.J.V. Anderson watches in amazement. *Derek Cross*

upon it unknown since the darkest days of World War 2. The Stranraer men took this in their stride and were most scathing about the efforts of Ayr crews on the occasional turns the latter worked to and from Stranraer. As one of the Skimming Brothers once told me, 'Yon Ayr men are too used to the flat roads tae Glesca, and when they see a hill it pits the fear o' God into them'. I say, 'the Skimming Brothers' as this tended to be another Stranraer tradition. Engine driving was a family tradition best sumed up in David Smith's immortal book *Tales of the Glasgow and South Western* (pub Ian Allan Ltd) when an inspector from head office in the despised 'Glesca' found that rules and procedures for protecting failed trains in single line sections were totally ignored. Just who the driver was, I am not certain, but the inspector involved in

the visit was informed to his considerable alarm that, 'On this road we ken where yuin and other are'. This was long before the days of extra-sensory perception, but they *did* 'ken where yuin and other were.' The Stranraer men were a very closely knit community: they had to be on these lonely, twisting lines on nights of black storm. The strange thing about the routes to Stranraer was that while they were as bleak and hard as any in Scotland, their trains were timed to run at far higher speeds, with far heavier trains, than on the better-known lines of the Highland Railway.

The former G&SW lines were without pity or mercy, either to the locomotives that worked over them, or the crews that drove the engines. I remember a remark made by Bob Smillie, now a senior Ayr driver, who booked on as a passed fireman during the war to fire on a 'Jubilee'. He said that when they got beyond Barrhill he thought they had fallen off the edge of the world. The Chirmorie was like that at night – there was eleven miles of nothingness. The Barrhill starting signal *could* have been the edge of the world. I know, as I have been on the footplate across these moors many times and there was nothing to show you that you were still in touch with the rest of the world. The occasional shepherd's cottage, perhaps, but shepherds went to bed early and, often as not, had no oil for their lamps anyhow. The 'High Chain' on the Port Road was much the same, mile upon mile of nothingness. You *could* have walked off the edge of the world. Small wonder, then, that Stranraer bred a unique breed of locomotive crews. It is less wonder that they tended to be wild men in a wilder landscape.

I had the luck to know and to travel with the last of the old school of Stranraer men brought up in the days of steam, and often pitifully underpowered steam at that. Jimmy Irvine I have already mentioned. The Skimming Brothers, one of whom, Jimmy I think, nearly caused me to drown at Bladnoch on the Whithorn branch one day. Having braved the notorious Solway tides to get a photograph of the thrice-weekly goods from Whithorn to Newton Stewart, as I waded ashore for safety, he appeared and asked if I could take him round by Wigton to buy some fags. I agreed, but then realised that he was supposed to be driving the train and that I had mislaid my eldest son, last seen getting on to the footplate at Whithorn. I asked Jimmy who was driving the train and was given a look implying that this was a stupid question. 'Why, ye're boy, of course. He *has* been all the way from Whithorn. . . he's no bad either'. This incident did have profitable results. It happened that shortly

afterwards a horse named 'Bladnoch Brig' was running in a race at Ayr. While I normally consider horses to be quadrupeds that bite at one end and kick at the other, I rashly hazarded 10/-(50p) on the nag. It was a rank outsider, but won at 20 to 1 – all the other horses having fallen over! Some days later, I met Skimming in Ayr who asked me if I had backed this cuddy. When I admitted I had, I was promptly accosted for a donation to the Stranraer pipe-band of which Jimmy Skimming was an ardent supporter. It was with Jimmy's brother (or cousin, as there were a lot of Skimmings at Stranraer at that time) that I had one of my two illicit footplate trips over the 'Port Road' back in 1951. This was when the 3.40pm Stranraer – Dumfries was a regular Compound job, among the last in South-West Scotland. By Stranraer's standards, the run was relatively uneventful, other than Andy's theory that if an 'injun' had three cylinders, then they should be used to the best effect. Old No 40919 was worked as a simple out of every station, at least if the start was level or uphill. It made for a splendid racket, but rather a rough ride.

My other footplate trip on the 'Port Road' was a tame affair with a driver whose surname I forget, but who was known as Ian. We had a good 'Black 5' and a light load. Apart from an altercation with the signalman at Loch Skerrow as to why he had not brought him a newspaper, the run included nothing remarkable, other than the driver informing that worthy that he would get a paper when he paid for the previous weeks and not before. Also, that Loch Skerrow might be noted for its fishing, but was equally good for signalmen to jump into!

It has all changed now. Rugs, tugs and breakaways with unfitted goods trains are a thing of the past. While the line is working to near capacity nowadays, all the freight traffic between Ayr and Stranraer is conveyed on air-braked Speedlink trains worked mainly by Class 40s making their last stand in Scotland. In this, there is a strange case of

Left:
15 April 1963: a day that patrons of an SLS rail tour of Galloway will not forget in a hurry. Bob McCann on the footplate of Kingmoor's 'pet' 'Jubilee' No 45588 *Kashmir,* **seen passing Stranraer Harbour Junction, en route Newton Stewart–Stranraer.** *Derek Cross*

Below left:
Departure from Girvan on 14 March 1963. Preserved GNSR 4-4-0 No 49 *Gordon Highlander* **and Highland Railway 'Jones Goods' 4-6-0 No 103 are working light to Stranraer, in preparation for return with a rail tour to Glasgow a couple of days later. One of the Skimmings and 'Booler' Marshall have relieved a Dawsholm crew at Ayr.** *Derek Cross*

Below:
'Grand injuin . . . it can *run*!' **McCann and mate on LMS '5' 4-6-0 No 44767 piloting No 45162 out of Girvan Goods in May 1966 with the 08.05 Stranraer–Falkland Junction fitted freight.** *Derek Cross*

history repeating itself. The old guard of Stranraer (and, to an extent, Ayr) drivers who worked that line in steam days swore by the '5Xs' ('Jubilees'), saying that they were far better engines for the lines than the '5s'. In view of the hilly nature of both Stranraer roads, this seems extraordinary, but their preference was ascribed to the more even torque of the three-cylinder engines. The Stranraer men, perverse as it may seem, tend to prefer the Class 40s to 47s for the heavy fitted freights of today, maintaining that while the former might be slower, they have a better grip on the banks. Also, the leading bogie of the 40 makes for better riding round the incessant curves. More has changed, apart from the banning of loose-coupled freights. The old guard of drivers from the steam era that I knew have all retired, with the exception of 'Booler' Marshall: so called as he is very keen on bowls. I never knew Marshall well, but he got hold of a friend of mine who was playing golf near Stranraer the other day, and said he had seen Michael and me taking numerous photographs during the summer and thought that 'Yon Mr Cross was fed up with diesels.' He added that I was a man who was always after the '5Xs'. In 'Booler's' opinion, they were the best engines that ever worked to Stranraer. Yes, Marshall is probably the last of the old school of Stranraer drivers. He is a 'runner' and when the day time Euston-Stranraer train had its Class 47 replaced by a Class 37 at Ayr, the start was of McCann standards.

A start of McCann standards. This may mean little outside Ayrshire and Galloway, but if ever a driver became a legend in his lifetime, then it was 'Bob' McCann of Stranraer. He was a man of many paradoxes and known as the 'Mad' McCann – a fact that he imparted to an Ayr driver who was piloting

him northwards on a Stranraer-Newcastle train one afternoon shortly before steam finished. Peter Sadler, the Ayr driver involved, and who had recently come to Ayr from Ardrossan, was slightly alarmed, to say the least. He was much more alarmed before they got to Ayr as McCann had two speeds. . . flat-out, or, with luck, stop. It so happened that I got a photograph of this train at the top of the Crosshill Bank and have seldom seen two engines (BR '4' 2-6-0 No 76096 and 'Clan' No 72007) being driven like it. Peter assured me later that all he was doing was trying to keep out of that maniac's way! McCann really inspired the title of this essay, for while Stranraer boasted many drivers wild, McCann was the wildest of them all. Strange to say, the best of the many McCann stories that have become a legend in Ayrshire railway history, although ascribed to McCann, may not have involved him at all. This was the day that the 12.30 pm Glasgow St Enoch – Stranraer express ran over 6ft of rail *that wasn't there* at Irvine. The permanent way boys were replacing some points and there had been a breakdown in communication. They had lifted 6ft of rail on one side of the points when the 12.30 pm appeared, going at a very high speed. The locomotive and coaches bounced along the chairs and, miraculously, nothing came off. This incident was hushed up, and the P Way inspector involved said that had the driver been any other than McCann, and the speed less than 70 mph, then the whole lot would have gone down the bank. One fact

emerges from this. The train was going far faster than the permitted limit through Irvine, and it was this that probably saved a major disaster. The other fact is that in those days the 12.30 pm was worked by Stranraer men; because it was going so hard everyone concerned assumed that McCann was the driver. As there was no damage, other than to some chairs, and as the P Way people were at fault, the legend stuck in the annals of local railway history. It was decided by all involved that the least said about this the better. Dear old G & SW, Authority ended and – ends – at Paisley. Some months ago, I was told that the driver was *not* McCann, but one of the other Stranraer 'drivers wild'. Such was McCann's reputation as a hard 'runner' that he has been credited with this notorious episode ever since. Thirty or so years later, I don't suppose the truth will ever be known, but that train must have presented a remarkable sight.

Even if McCann has been falsely accused of the Irvine episode, it was a case of giving a dog a bad name. He was a hard 'runner', as they say in these parts. I know this to my cost. Many years ago,

Below:
'The Closeburn Incident'. Bob McCann has transferred to LMS '5' No 45160 which with Caprotti BR '5' 4-6-0 No 73134 is backing on to the down 'Northern Irishman' at Ayr on 30 July 1965. BR/Sulzer Type 4 No D34 has been removed from the train to the old Dalmellington branch platform and Inspector Tom Gibson 'guards' the diesel. *Derek Cross*

before I knew the man or his reputation, I had my one and only run in the cab of an unrebuilt 'Patriot' from Ayr to Stranraer. Once over the summit at Chirmorie, McCann was letting rip and dust and coal were flying all over the place. The firemen turned to me and said that they 'Wee Scots' (as the 'Patriots' were known) were awfully dirty engines. He got the stony reply, 'Then pit the hose on it, ye silly so and so!' After that, we proceeded to Stranraer in silence, but at a rather increased pace. On another occasion, a sudden thunderstorm caused me to bolt for shelter in Girvan station as a relief train to the north-east of England came down the Glendoune bank like a falling star and stopped for water in Girvan. Whereupon, the guard came up and informed McCann in words that do not bear repetition in a book for family reading that he (the guard) 'didn'a mind a bit of hard running to make up time, but for a great many people's sake, varying from the saviour to the devil, and all sorts between, McCann should, 'Gang roound they curves and nae cut across them.'

I had a similar experience with Bob McCann on the descent of the Glendoune Bank. In the winter of 1965/66, there was a fitted freight from Stranraer to Falkland Jn (Ayr) that was invariably double headed and a good candidate for 'chasing.' This particular morning I had photographed the train at Pinmore and was game for another couple of shots. At the Girvan waterworks, the line curves above the road on a high embankment, and I realised that, apart from the fitted vans, there were 15/16 empty coal wagons dancing about at the rear. I stopped as I assumed they would come cascading down the embankment. They didn't as it happened, but by the time I reached Girvan the pilot was taking water. Grinning out of the cab of the train engine was McCann. 'Oh, I beat ye this mornin', Mr Cross.' He never used my Christian name, unlike most of the Stranraer men. 'Yes', I said, 'I had to stop at the waterworks as I thought the empty wagons were coming down the bank on to the road.' 'What empty wagons?', said McCann. I didn't have time to answer before the guard, a thoroughly shaken man, came up and informed both drivers that he had experienced a very rough ride indeed, If his ride had been rough, then his language was rougher. The driver of the pilot was an Ayr man noted as being a hard 'runner'. Some days later, I asked him why they had taken so long from Pinmore to Girvan and got the answer that the Stranraer man was holding back all the way. Now, if ever there was a case of the pot calling the kettle sooty, this was it. Hugh was frightened of neither God nor Mammon, though he has a keen appreciation of the latter.

Yet, there was this strange anachronism about Bob McCann. I have spoken to many of the signalmen down the Stranraer Road and they said that, wild though he might be, he would never let them down. If Bob reckoned that he could not make the next crossing-place without holding up something more important, then he would not go. His theory was that the signalman should not get the blame for his performance. During the summer of 1965, Ayr, or Stranraer, got hold of the Stephenson valve gear 'Black 5' No 44767. Having been well and truly beaten from Barnhill to Girvan by McCann, he greeted me with the classic remark, 'Grand injuin this, boy, it can *run*'. If Bob said an 'injuin' could run then it could have won the Derby several years in a row.

Early on Friday 30 July 1965, while on my way to photograph trains on Shap, I called at Ayr station to beg, borrow or steal a Special Traffic Notice. Tom Gibson, at that time one of the station inspectors, told me that the 'Paddy' from Euston-Stranraer had failed at Closeburn, north of Dumfries. This was not long after the train had been altered to run via Annbank and Ayr following the closure of the 'Port Road'. Tom revealed that the train was being hauled by one of the big diesels off the 'Condor' London-Glasgow fitted freight and they had two steam locomotives waiting to replace it at Ayr. In the light of a summer's dawn 'Peak' No D34 duly arrived in Ayr with the 'Paddy' – by this time late, but not as far behind as I expected. It gave rise to one of the most spectacular photographs I have ever taken, as well as nearly causing a nervous breakdown on the part of poor Tom Gibson, who retired shortly afterwards. In came D34 with no less than the redoubtable McCann in charge. Most of the Stranraer men were 'passed' for driving diesel multiple-units and diesel locomotives of what became Classes 20 and 27, but they were certainly *not* 'passed' on 'Peaks'.

Even the replacement locomotives on hand at Ayr for the 'Paddy' were not entirely what I would have expected. The train engine was No 45160, the best 'Black 5' allocated to Ayr but the pilot was a Caprotti BR Standard '5', No 73134 that Ayr had 'borrowed' from Patricroft – without the latter's knowledge — to help out with the summer traffic. McCann was most reluctant to relinquish D34, but was finally ordered off by Tom Gibson after a heated altercation on the platform. The train duly departed for Stranraer with Nos 73134 and 45160 in charge and D34 was parked in the old Dalmellington platform to wait until someone who *was* passed to drive 'Peaks' could remove it. McC was not at all amused by this, and the start out of Ayr was spectacular, to say the least. I am not sure of the identity of the Ayr driver, but I think it was Alec Barron who also had the reputation of being a hard 'runner'. My wife maintains to this day that she heard the engines attacking the climb to Dalrymple Junction from six miles away. She assumed, as wives will, that I had decided to go to Stranraer and not to Shap.

The real cream of the joke came some weeks later when I was at Thornhill. Between trains, I was bidden by the signalman to his box for a cup of tea. We talked of various things and then it came out: 'The Closeburn Incident'. Right enough, the 'Paddy' headed by a 'Britannia' *had* failed at Closeburn. As the 'Condor' fitted freight from Brent to Glasgow was hard on its tail, they took the 'Peak' off the 'Condor' and put it on the 'Paddy'. The Carlisle man warned the good McCann that he would have to allow plenty of time to 'blow off' the brakes. This sensible advice was ignored, and the 'Paddy' set off for Stranraer before the brakes were released. Full power and no trimmings – there never were with McCann! I will leave it to the signalman at Thornhill to describe the scene. 'It was a lovely, calm summer's morn', Mr Cross, nae a breath o' wind. I kent what had happened at Closeburn and that they were changing injuins. Then I saw it, aye, and *heard* it! I hae never heard a loco being worked like it, but it was the sparks from they brakes. . . man, it was better than Guy Fawkes night!'

Not all the Stranraer drivers were 'drivers wild'. . . it was the saner ones who stood out as being the eccentrics! Willy Whannel, for instance, had the theory that rules were rules and timetables for the keeping thereof. If he left five minutes late, he arrived five minutes late. Like all the old brigade he has retired now, but he accosted me one day on Ayr station and informed me that, 'Ye're friend McCann is off the road'. My answer was 'Not again'. I got the astonishing answer that, 'It's his heid! When I laughed, I was told in stentorian terms that, 'They medics in Glesca have found there was something wrang wi his heid'. He added that he, W.W., thought it was result of 20 years of McCann's own driving. I took this with about half an hundred-weight of salt until the redoubtable Jimmy Irvine informed me that McC was on the harbour pilot as he was 'off the main line'. Since Jimmy was the one man in Stranraer who could give Bob McCann a start and a beating when it came to fast running, I didn't take this very seriously. Then it happened. I drove to Stranraer to meet a friend from off the evening ferry from Larne and there, having obviously run out of rail (indeed, one of them was teetering over the storm-tossed waters of Loch Ryan) were a couple of parcels vans. The yardmaster was wringing his hands saying that since McCann was on the pilot he had never had an evening's peace. It was all unfair as McCann suffered a minor stroke soon after and was confined to a wheelchair. Even then, Stranraer's 'black' humour prevailed as one of the drivers (who must remain nameless) told me that if I was in Stranraer and saw a wheelchair taking the corners on one wheel then I'd know who was driving it! It is of such stories that legends are born, and if there was ever a legend then it was Bob McCann.

But the G&SW traditions have lived on to the present day. The Railfair exhibition of steam locomotives and modern traction held at Ayr on 29/30 October 1983 has added to the legends. First, *Flying Scotsman* worked an enthusiasts' excursion from Annan to Ayr the previous weekend, and in the hands of G&SW section men, roared through the New Cumnock at something over 60 mph with 12 coaches on *against* the grade. I have never heard a locomotive make a roar like it. As the exhibits were being assembled at Ayr before the celebrated weekend, the BR Class 08 diesel shunter packed up, and the preserved North British 0-6-0 *Maude* was quickly substituted and produced some extraordinary sound-effects when propelling a rake of 'dead' locomotives including *Flying Scotsman* and the preserved 'Deltic' No 55.002. Another highlight was that on the day after the Railfair, some of the fitters at Ayr got No 55.002 working, and there was a plot to work it back to Carlisle *at the head* of a Stranraer-Tyne Yard Speedlink train. Alas, none of the Ayr men was passed for 'Deltics' and a request to Haymarket for a driver was intercepted by the HQ at Buchanan House, saying that the locomotive had gone to the National Railway Museum as unserviceable. . . and that was the way it had to stay. In fact, the 'Deltic' is in full working order, so officialdom had a close shave!

'A4' No 60009 *Union of South Africa* reached Ayr for the Railfair weekend on an enthusiasts' excursion. A Stranraer man, who was working a rather feeble Class 27 diesel locomotive following the 'A4' into Ayr, insisted that he should fail the '27' and, 'Tak yon injuin instead', adding that the 'A4' was facing Stranraer anyhow, and 'had a good heid o' steam'. I wonder what Pinmore Tunnel would have done to the 'A4' or, come to that, the other way about?

It is quite extraordinary just how wide is the circulation of *Railway World Annuals*. In the 1984 *Annual,* I wrote about my trip to Nepal in the late 1950s, and the fact that I was provided with a rifle (to shoot tigers with) when chasing one of that country's steam locomotives. Charlie McArthur, now a Kingmoor driver, but formerly of Dumfries, accosted me the other day, saying. 'Aye, it's pity that ye hadn'a a rifle at the Big Fleet Viaduct when ye tried to help that adder oot its skin!' Old sins last long, especially in this part of Scotland.

London Transport review
Photo feature

London Transport has been seldom out of the news in the last decade, but much of the controversy has concerned its control and management. Railway enthusiasts at large have tended to find British Rail's operations of more interest, but there is a loyal following for LT's surface and deep-level tube rolling stock, services and stations. Our review provides a brief glance at the diversity of environments served by LT trains, and the changes in rolling stock in the last few years.

The changing scene:
Right:
The 1983 Tube Stock now being delivered will help displace the remaining trains of 1938 Tube Stock on the Bakerloo Line. In 1982, Bakerloo Line peak-hour trains were withdrawn north of Stonebridge Park. A train of 1938 Tube Stock waits at Watford Junction in 1978. *R.L. Sewell*

Far right:
The D stock saw the end of the last surface stock of prewar inspiration, the R class, finally withdrawn in 1983. Two R class trains pass at West Kensington on 8 June 1978. *Kevin Lane*

Below right:
With commendable enterprise, LT has made available former Metropolitan Railway Bo-Bo electric locomotive No 12 *Sarah Siddons* for enthusiasts' rail tours and it has appeared also at BR Open Days. On 5 September 1982, at the head of BR Mk 2 stock, No 12 comes out of the subway from Neasden depot before working a special. *Brian Stephenson*

Below:
LT contrasts at Earls Court, 1983. A train of D stock, with its functional, sleek features provides a counterpoint to train information displays. *John G. Glover*

35

Right:
Victoria Line 1967 Tube Stock trains are not often photographed in the open air. One such train waits at the LT staff platform at Northumberland Park depot on 29 August 1979. *R.E. Ruffell*

Below:
The Epping–Ongar line has survived a closure proposal, and now works at peak-hours only. At North Weald, a four-car set of 1962 Tube Stock passes LT's only remaining semaphore signals, when heading for Ongar on 22 July 1977. *John G. Glover*

Bottom:
A Metropolitan Line Hammersmith–Whitechapel train, made up of C77 stock, approaches Paddington on 1 June 1981. *Colin J. Marsden*

BR in the 1970s
Photo feature

If the previous decade had seen the disappearance of steam in regular service on BR, the 1970s were of interest, not only for the elimination of many of the other survivals of earlier motive power developments, but for the establishment of the modern face of our national railway system. Regrettably, many projected developments, such as the Advanced Passenger Train or extensive main line electrification, were destined to pass into the 1980s with no firm expectation of their realisation.

Below:
Most problematic of the hopes for a golden age for British Rail is the Advanced Passenger Train. One high-spot of its gestation was the successful trial running at over 150mph with the APT-E (experimental) gas turbine train. Here it is moving at high speed between Goring and Pangbourne on a trial run from Swindon on 24 July 1975.
D.E. Canning

15

Still the mainstay of the diesel fleet in the 1970s were two classes of main line diesel locomotive, scheduled for withdrawal in the 1980s:

Above:

Class 40 No 40.100 (since withdrawn) heads a Manchester—Newcastle parcels train at York on 4 February 1978. *D.J. Hayes*

Below:

Class 45 No 45.056 pases Ferryhill, under a stormy sky, with the 11.39 Poole—Newcastle of 19 July 1977. *G. Lake*

Tell-tale signs that this is a scene from the 1970s are the train headcode worn by Class 86/2 No 86.209 (now named *City of Coventry*) and the presence of Class 50 No 50.022 (now on the Western Region). The train is the overnight Glasgow–Manchester (now withdrawn), and the place, Carlisle, in 1976.
A. Swain

Electric sunset: rolling stock from 1930s electrification schemes gave way to new working in the 1970s, such as the Manchester South Junction and Altrincham 1,500V dc units; this section of line was converted to 25V ac.

Left:
One of the 1931 units (left) forms the 16.10 to Altrincham at Manchester Oxford Road on 21 January 1971, four months before withdrawal.

Below left:
The much loved 'Brighton Belle' was withdrawn in 1972, and the rolling stock passed to preservation. The 11.00 down service to Brighton climbs Grosvenor Bank out of Victoria on 29 June 1971. *J.H. Cooper-Smith*

From one age . . . to another.

Above:
The big event of the 1970s, in terms of displaced motive power, was the withdrawal of the main line diesel hydraulic locomotives. Class 52 No 1049 *Western Monarch* enjoys rapt attention at Solihull when working the 10.25 Birmingham New Street–Paddington of 6 January 1976. *Philip D. Hawkins*

Below:
It was no small shock to see ICI25 units lined up side by side, such as at Paddington on 9 August 1977, a year after their general introduction to WR InterCity service. A Class 31 'intrudes', far right. *Brian Morrison*

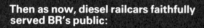

Then as now, diesel railcars faithfully served BR's public:

Above:
A Class 124 unit near Huddersfield with the 11.10 Liverpool Lime St–Hull of 12 March 1979; these were shortly to be displaced from the Diggle route by loco-hauled workings. *Mrs D.A. Robinson*

Below:
Two Class 117 units at Par on 30 July 1979, in-between Newquay line workings. *D.J. Hayes*

Although the 'Deltics' were not all withdrawn until the end of 1981, they bowed out on the East Coast route's premier trains in the late 1970s. So did Pullman cars. The up 'Yorkshire Pullman' passes Wood Green on 5 April 1978 behind Class 55 No 55.002 *The King's Own Yorkshire Light Infantry* (since preserved). *R.G. Avery*

Derby lightweight railcars
Photo feature

Thirty years ago, the first quantity production diesel railcars went into service on BR. They became known as the Derby lightweight railcars – alloy construction was used to reduce vehicle weight, such that the motor brakes were 4–10 tons lighter than subsequent designs. Powered by two British United Traction (AEC) six-cylinder horizontal engines, these railcars set the standard for over 4,000 vehicles built under the Modernisation Plan of 1955. However, the first eight two-car sets had hydro-mechanical transmission with Lysholm-Smith torque converters to the final drive. The other sets had the conventional cardan shaft drive to a four-speed gearbox and to the final drive.

The Derby lightweight sets went into traffic on the Eastern and London Midland Region as two-car sets working in the West Riding of Yorkshire, the Manchester area, West Cumberland, Lincolnshire and East Anglia. Five four-car units were allocated to the North Eastern Region for Middlesbrough–Newcastle services. All units to this design were in service by 1956, and were among the first BR standard railcars to be withdrawn, some lasting only 5–7 years in traffic. A few vehicles have survived in departmental use.

Other odd men out in the railcars of this design were the pair of motor brake seconds capable of working singly, and used from Bletchley on Banbury–Buckingham and other lines.

Above:
A typical brochure issued in connection with the inauguration of railcar working.

Below:
One of the NER four-car sets, when new. Note the stylish front-end design which regrettably was not adopted for later railcar types.   *BR*

Left:
Early days of dieselisation. A Boston—Grantham train at Rauceby station.
T.G. Hepburn/Rail Archive Stephenson

Below left:
A rare picture of one of the single unit cars, M79900, working with a motor composite from a twin unit, at Potton on a Bletchley—Cambridge train, 16 April 1966. The Derby lightweight cars could only be worked with their own type — coded yellow triangle — a fact that contributed to their early demise.
P.R. Foster

Below:
Formerly cars Nos M 79018/79612, and now the BR ultrasonic test train, DB 975007 (leading) and 975008, seen at Twickenham on 10 September 1974.
J. Scrace

Bottom:
Test coach *Iris* RDB 975010 is used for radio and train control experimental work. This was formerly M 79900 seen above. Painted in red and blue, *Iris* was photographed at Swindon Works in November 1975. *Brian Morrison*

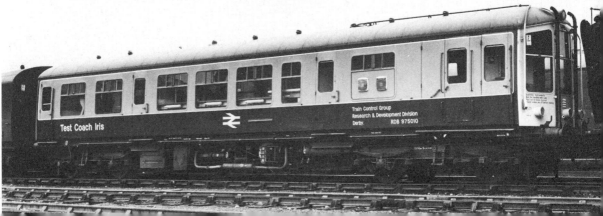

Coal and British railways
Photo feature

The need to transport coal from mine to industrial and private users gave birth to the British railway system. In the next few pages, we take a look at colliery systems and main line movements of coal, reflecting on changing patterns of working.

Below:
The last National Coal Board colliery in England to make regular use of steam locomotives was Bickershaw, near Wigan where it was retained on stand-by into the 1980s. Two Hunslet 0-6-0STs are seen in action on 15 April 1977. *L.A. Nixon*

The Scottish NCB collieries dispensed with the regular working of steam locomotives in the 1970s. One of the most attractive latter-day survivals was the Waterside system, in Ayrshire.

Right:
NCB West Ayr No 1 (AB 2368/55) takes refreshment at Waterside in March 1978.

Below right:
West Ayr No 21 (AB 2284/49) heads a train from Dunaskin for the tip, in September 1973.
Both: Joe Rajczonek

Above left:
Steam remained on coal workings in the north-east until 1967. Ryhope Colliery was due to close shortly after 'J27' 0-6-0 No 65872 was photographed there on 31 October 1966. *I.S. Carr*

Left:
But even with dieselisation, patterns of working often remained unchanged. Goole Yard is seen in June 1974, with lines of wagons loaded with coal for export. *BR*

Above:
Probably the swansong of steam operations at a colliery occurred unexpectedly in late 1981 when Hunslet 0-6-0ST (3168/44) was ostensibly on trial at Wheldale Colliery, near Castleford. But the experiment, if such it was, was short-lived, and the engine then departed for preservation. It is seen blasting away from the ash-dump at Wheldale, with empties for the washery in December 1981.
Brian Dobbs

The new order – Class 56 No 56.076 (now named *Blyth Power*) keeps on the move with a train of HBA hopper wagons forming a merry-go-round service from a north-east pit. The coal is being emptied into the rapid discharge point at Blyth power station on 18 May 1982.   *Peter J. Robinson*

Coal working old-style in the 1980s:

Left:
May 1984 was the 'cut-off' date for the conversion of wagonload traffic on BR, and so trains of 16ton 'Mins' such as these empties from East Anglia belong to the past. Class 20s Nos 20.171/20.140 are near Ashwell, on the Peterborough—Leicester line, with the 13.55 Whitemoor—Toton class '8' train of 21 April 1983. *John C. Baker*

Below:
The rationalisation of NCB pits, combined with BR's new styles of working, will put an end to scenes like this at Cynheidre Colliery, near Llanelli. Class 37 No 37.251 positions wagons on 16 June 1983.
Tom Heavyside

Right:
The future: BR's new freight workhorse — the Class 58 — No 58.002 of which is heading the 10.01 Mantle Lane—Drakelow power station merry-go-round train at Drakelow East Curve on 11 November 1983.
A.O. Wynn

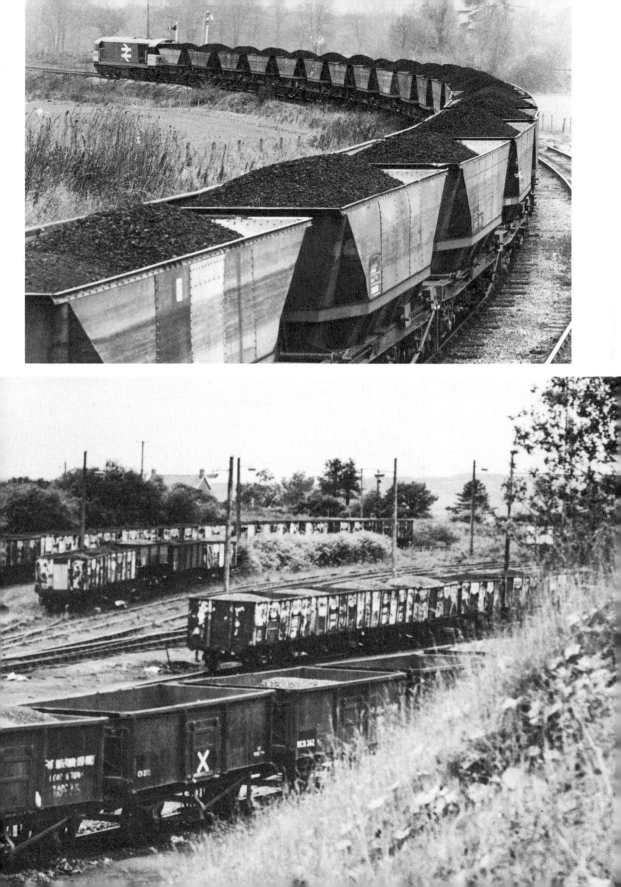

Trains and signals
Photo feature

Only seldom can the combination of lineside colour light signals and trains approach the attractiveness of semaphore signalling with trains. The importance of signals to a photographer in composing a picture may be apparent from these six pages.

Below:
LMS 'Royal Scot' 4-6-0 No 6115 *Scots Guardsman* **at the familiar location of Chinley North Junction, signalled for the Hope Valley route with the 'Yorkshire Venturer' charter train of 11 November 1978.**
Allan Stewart

Top right:
Great Westernry at Bridgnorth, Severn Valley Railway on 12 October 1980. '2251' 0-6-0 No 3205 sets off light engine, bound for Bewdley.
W. A. Sharman

Bottom right:
Without mechanical signalling and the signalbox this would be a characterless view—looking north from Wellingborough station on 9 November 1978. A Class 47 on the down slow lines with a tanker train.
W. A. Sharman

Above:
Mechanical signalling at London termini will soon be a memory. This is Charing Cross, South Eastern & Chatham Railway, with its signalbox spanning the tracks, and seen in the years before 1914.
LPC/Ian Allan Library

Right:
The 'bobby' in his box of polished levers and block instruments, keeping a careful eye on passing trains, is replaced by a centralised power signalbox where movements are watched on panels. Signalman D.E. Canning works the now-replaced Midgham box, on the Berks and Hants line.   *Neil Giles*

The disappearing scene:

Above:
Class 37 No 37.246 passes Masborough South Junction with a block load of steel, heading towards Chesterfield on 25 July 1978. The semaphore signalling was replaced, and track layout rationalised during the following month.   *T. Dodgson*

Left:
Not only semaphore signals at Whitchurch (Salop), but a water column is still in situ on 8 April 1978.
M.R. Henney

Below left:
The West of England resignalling train passes Blatchbridge Junction signalbox on 23 April 1983 watched by the signalman. This signalbox disappeared under the Westbury (Wilts) mas scheme.   *Peter W. Durham*

Left:
The preserved railways will become museums for mechanical signalling. 'Jubilee' 4-6-0 No 5690 *Leander* **leaves Goathland for Pickering on 7 July 1983 and approaches some fine North Eastern Railway signals.** *J.H. Cooper-Smith*

Above:
The once-familiar GWR lower quadrant signals are becoming rare. BR '9F' 2-10-0 No 92220 *Evening Star* **takes the 'Welsh Marches Pullman' out of Shrewsbury for Hereford on 17 April 1982.** *W.A. Sharman*

Recalling East African steam

Rev Robert de Berry

I FIRST fell in love with East African Railways in 1961. At that time, I was granted a footplate pass on an EAR '60' Class 4-8-2/2-8-4 Garratt from Nakuru in Kenya, to Kampala, the capital of Uganda. The long train drew into Kampala, more than 800 miles from its starting-point at Mombasa, at exactly noon – not a minute late.

Until the mid-1970s, EAR was still intact, and despite the influx of diesel locomotives from GEC/ 'English Electric,' Canada and West Germany, steam continued to play a significant role in the system's operations in Kenya, Tanzania and Uganda. In any case, there was always a lapse of time between deliveries of new diesels and replacements of steam, particularly as some of the new arrivals were none too reliable. In 1974, my wife and I travelled from Kampala to Dar Es Salaam – 1,172 miles – in 71 hours; from Voi to Moshi and from Moshi to Dar Es Salaam. The '60' class Garratts were at the head of our trains. Most of the freight traffic between Mombasa and Nairobi was in the hands of the giant '59' Class 4-8-2/2-8-4 Garratts; indeed, this remained the case until 1978/ 79. By 1974, steam had only been totally eliminated between Nakuru and Jinja, Tororo and Soroti, on the branch lines to Solai, Kitale and Thompson Falls and on the long, 'waterless' branch to Magadi. In Tanzania, most of the Central line had been dieselised, but the lines to Tanga, Moshi and Arusha were entirely steam, as were those to Mpanda, Mwanza and Kigoma.

East African Railways and Harbours, as an integrated system serving Kenya, Uganda and Tanzania, are no more; each country now runs its railway as an internal network. Orders for the supply of new locomotives have been fulfilled, as

Below:
One of the standard light Garratts used on the erstwhile East African Railways system, '60' 4-8-2 + 2-8-4 No 6004 (one of 12 built by Franco-Belge), on a Nairobi–Dar Es Salaam train photographed in Tanzania during August 1974. *Rev Robert de Berry*

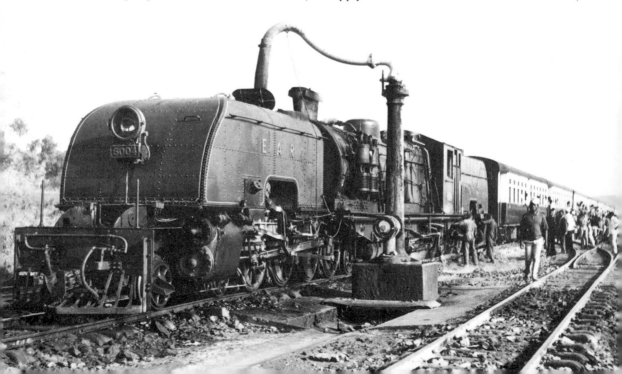

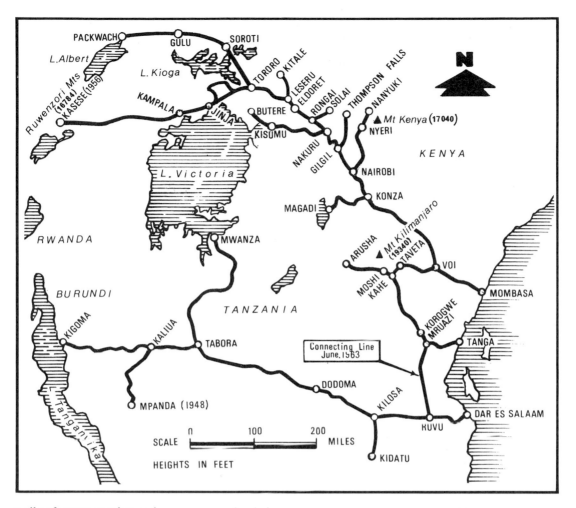

well as for new coaches and wagons, a number being produced in British Rail Engineering Ltd workshops. The trains that formerly went from Voi to Moshi, now terminate at Taveta; there are in any case few of them. The one-time daily Mombasa-Kampala Mail train now works thrice-weekly from Nairobi to the Ugandan border at Malabar. The political separation of the East African countries has rendered a once profitable and efficient railway network an easy prey to competition from road transport. As evidence, the constant line of heavy lorries labouring up from the coast to and through Uganda is a vigorous illustration of the lack of importance of the railway today.

By 1980, despite the delivery of 26 new '93' Class diesel locomotives from General Electric of the USA, 56 '62' Class B-Bs from Henschel and some of the 35 '47' Class shunters from Britain (Hunslet/BREL), some steam remained at work in Kenya. Most of these engines were on shunting duties, while a large number of main line locomotives were on shed out of use. Occasional steam workings

Above:
Unkempt '31' 2-8-4 No 3110 *Bakiga* **outside Nairobi shed on 2 August 1979.**   *P.J. Howard*

63

remained at Voi and a '31' 2-8-4 laboured up to Taveta from time to time. At Mombasa, there were disused steam locomotives, although there were hints of occasional workings. At Kisumu, local turns were still steam worked, usually by '24' 4-8-0s and '31' 2-8-4s. The Kisumu line was the original section of the former turn of the century Uganda Railway. Uganda was always the goal of the original railway-builders, Kenya being viewed as a barren stepping-stone to the 'Pearl of Africa'. Sadly, the train ferries which used to operate from Kisumu to Jinja on Lake Victoria, no longer carry freight wagons. However, Kisumu's passenger traffic had increased by the mid-1970s and there were often two long night-time trains to Nairobi. Until the same period there was the night-time all-class train, and a third-class only daytime train between Nakuru and Nairobi.

To round off the story of Kenya's steam power, by 1983 only one steam locomotive was still at work, and that unofficially – No 2416 at Kisumu. However, no less than 24 locomotives were still at Nairobi depot, almost all complete. Time will tell if any of them return to service, perhaps on tourist steam specials.

Returning to my visit in 1980, when we went into Uganda, I didn't know what to expect. When my wife and I had begun work in Soroti in 1971, steam was supreme. Although the 'English Electric' 2,025hp '87' Class and 1,350hp '71' Class worked up from Kenya to Kampala, no shed in Uganda had a diesel allocation. In 1972, Tororo, near the Kenyan

Above:
'59' Class 4-8-2 + 2-8-4 Beyer Garratt No 5931 *Uluguru Mountains* **at Konza, working an up freight from Mombasa on 13 December 1976.** *Hugh Ballantyne*

Above right:
The fireman overdoes things on '59' 4-8-2 + 2-8-4 Garratt No 5918 *Mount Gelai* **at work in Kenya during 1978. Note the Giesl ejector. This engine has been preserved.** *Mike Wood*

Below right:
'24' 4-8-0 No 2431 photographed at Achuna, operating from Soroti towards Lira in April 1972. *Rev Robert de Berry*

border, was dieselised, using 'English Electric' and Henschel locomotives. By 1974, diesel traction was working north of Soroti to Gulu, but the rarely-worked Gulu-Packwach section remained steam. Gulu still had half a dozen '24' 4-8-0s, but a derailment in 1978 ended their operations and the Gulu-Packwach section remains unopened.

In April/May 1979, President Amin was mercifully overthrown. His departing troops killed 200 people on a train at Soroti and the line remained almost closed until a sevice was re-established on 3 January 1980 – a twice weekly train runs from Tororo-Gulu. Traffic between Kenya and Uganda was, however, minimal. Six times a week, a mixed train operated between Tororo and Kampala. Political differences between Kenya and Uganda, and ties between Uganda and Tanzania, meant that

Rare photographs of the twilight of steam in Uganda:

Top:
Redundant '60' class Garratts at Kampala shed.

Above:
'31' 2-8-4 No 3109 inside Kampala shed. This locomotive was later returned to steam. Both photographs were taken on 11 January 1980 by Rev Robert de Berry.

Below:
'24' 4-8-0 No 2431 about to depart from Soroti, Uganda with the delayed 09.30 freight to Gulu, in January 1972. *Rev Robert de Berry*

freight was routed via the train ferries operating from Jinja to Mwanza. By 1980, the fleet of diesel locomotives in Uganda included a number of unserviceable units although replacements were on order from Germany and France. India was supplying passenger coaches and wagons.

I inevitably headed for Kampala locomotive shed, wondering what I would find. There were seven redundant '60' class Garratts, but two were in good condition. Apparently, one had worked freight to Jinja in July 1979, and another had reached Kasese that October. But it was doubtful if they would operate again; the Kasese line was dieselised with '62' class Henschels delivered in 1978. The other engines at Kampala were all '31' 2-8-4s, and the shedmaster hoped to have No 3109 on the road later in January 1980, to be followed by No 3137. The rest mostly looked derelict. Indeed, the shed itself was little better and the roof, in poor condition.

At the time, Kasese, 208 miles to the west of Kampala, had the only operating steam locomotives in Uganda. The shedmaster was in Kampala to locate spare parts for two of his six '31' class allocation from among Kampala's unserviceable examples. At Kasese, two '31s' were in steam, there were the two awaiting repair, and the other pair were beyond redemption. Steam was retained for shunting wagons up the two-mile siding to the copper mine, for engineering and water trains, and for working the seven-mile branch from the Kasese line to a cement works. The shedmaster told me that he needed four workable engines. We stood and chatted as we looked at a line of redundant products from Beyer Peacock and Vulcan Foundry.

Even with dieselisation, the railways of East Africa continue to provide interesting travelling, and the first main line diesel locomotives, the '87' class built by 'English Electric', perform with a hardiness and reputation for first-rate performance that is pleasing. And there is always the splendid Nairobi Railway Museum to visit!.

Brian Morrison – steam cameraman
Photo feature

I live in the south-east of England, and the opportunities for main line steam photography do not occur very often. Apart from the two Paddington extravaganzas – the 125th anniversary of the station in March 1979, and the shuttle trips to the Old Oak Common Traction Maintenance Depot in September 1981 – the south-east based photographer generally needs to make lengthy journeys so as to keep abreast of the current steam preservation scene.

The steam locomotive attracted me to photography in the early 1950s, and its virtual demise in the mid-1960s correspondingly prompted my loss of interest. But during a holiday in North Wales in the 1970s, a steam railway awakened my interest once more, with the sight, sound and aroma of steam. In short, it relit my fire!

These days, I am probably better-known as a modern traction photographer, but I still expend quite a lot of film on the steam engine. When unable to view main line specials, at least I have the excellent consolation of the south-east's steam lines, such as the Kent & East Sussex, Bluebell, Mid-Hants and several others.

There is no doubt that the steam scene is nothing like it was in my early days of railway photography, but the fact that steam can still be enjoyed is a tribute to all those involved in steam preservation in the past two decades.

Above:
On a damp April morning in 1982, Adams '0415' 4-4-2T No 488 steams away from Sheffield Park station, Bluebell Railway with a members' special for Horsted Keynes.

All photographs pages 67–74 by Brian Morrison

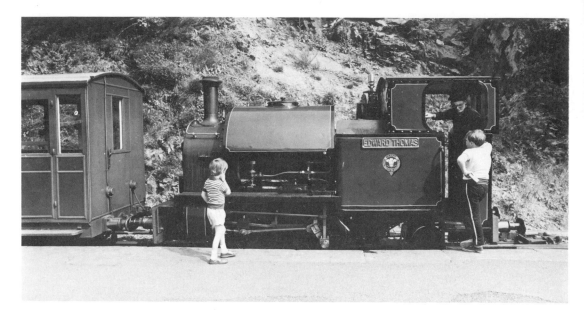

Contrasts in steam preservation in Wales:

Above:
Young enthusiasts are fascinated by the Talyllyn's Kerr Stuart 0-4-2ST No 4 *Edward Thomas* at Abergynolwyn, ready to depart for Tywyn on 2 June 1978. This is an instance where a wide-angle lens proved beneficial: there was insufficient room to move further backwards to record the scene with a standard lens.

Below:
In an attractive sylvan setting on the approaches to Llangollen station, Kitson 0-6-0ST (5459/32) operates the steam shuttle to/from the renovated station on 13 September 1981.

Bleak conditions on the Settle & Carlisle line:

Right:
'A4' 4-6-2 No 4498 *Sir Nigel Gresley* makes a stirring sight near Ribblehead with a northbound 'Cumbrian Mountain Express' on 19 January 1980.

Below right:
In particularly cold weather on 5 February 1983, the scheduled watering of the locomotives at Hellifield was greatly delayed as the hoses of the fire brigade tender were frozen. Eventually, the northbound 'Cumbrian Mountain Pullman' left 1½hrs late, and this photograph of the train pulling away from Hellifield is a tribute to modern fast lenses and film emulsions. The motive power consists of Midland Compound 4-4-0 No 1000 and 'Jubilee' 4-6-0 No 5690 *Leander.*

BR-built locomotives in action:

Above left:
Carrying an 81A (Old Oak Common) shed plate for the occasion, '9F' 2-10-0 No 92220 *Evening Star* leaves Paddington and passes under Ranelagh Road bridge on 20 September 1981, with the first special of the day to Old Oak Common. The event commemorated the 75th anniversary of the depot.

Above:
BR '4' 2-6-4T No 80135 is given dramatic treatment by a 300mm lens as it emerges from Grosmont Tunnel with a Pickering train on the North Yorkshire Moors Railway, 26 May 1980.

Left:
Ivatt '4' 2-6-0 No 43106 works from Dorridge to Didcot with a special and passes under the canal aqueduct between Warwick and Leamington Spa on 11 April 1981. A narrow boat has stopped above to watch the proceedings!

Contrast in tank engines:

Above right:
A typical scene on the Kent & East Sussex Railway: shortly after New Mill bridge was reopened in September 1977, it is crossed by Hunslet 0-6-0ST No 24 (since renamed *William H. Austen*) with a train from Tenterden towards Wittersham Road.

Right:
'14xx' 0-4-2T No 1450 *Ashburton* steams away from Staverton Bridge, Dart Valley Railway on 1 July 1979 and heads towards Totnes Riverside.

Above:
Silhouetted against the dipping sun on a fine April day in 1977, LMS '5' 4-6-0 No 45110 *RAF Biggin Hill* **crosses the Severn Valley Railway's Victoria Bridge, Arley with a train from Foley Park to Bridgnorth. Only a couple of decades earlier, so many of this class could be found that it had to be something special for me to bother to photograph one!**

Contrasts in '8P' motive power:

Left:
It is ten years since the last steam special ran on the Southern Region. On 27 April 1974, rebuilt 'Merchant Navy' 4-6-2 No 35028 *Clan Line* **makes a fine sight as it rounds the curve at Battledown, west of Worting Junction, with a special from Basingstoke to Westbury.**

Below:
Passing Bayston Hill, south of Shrewsbury, 'King' 4-6-0 No 6000 *King George V* **storms uphill towards Hereford with the 'Midland Jubilee' special of 1 October 1977.**

Above:
Restored to its South Eastern & Chatham Railway livery, Wainwright 'H' 0-4-4T No 263 has just arrived at Horsted Keynes, Bluebell Railway with the 'Night Mail' special of 17 October 1981. As there was very little light falling on the scene from the station, the camera shutter was left open for 30 sec and, using a hand-held flash gun, I walked about to illuminate the scene satisfactorily.

Below:
At the end of a beautifully sunny day in May 1977, 'A4' 4-6-2 No 60009 *Union of South Africa* is caught at speed near Blackford, between Perth and Stirling, with the return 'Silver Jubilee Special' to Kirkcaldy. The train was very late and the sun had already sunk behind the Glenalmond Hills.

Return to Dorchester South – 1961

S. A. Rocksborough Smith

I STILL have the return half of my ticket, Dorchester South to Surbiton via Sway, dated 15 July 1961. When I was arranging my week's holiday, the family were surprised that I chose to travel there and back on a Saturday, the busiest day of the week. But I never thought twice about it, and the choice of train was equally obvious: the 9.25am Saturdays only Wimbledon to Weymouth, leaving Surbiton at 9.34.

I arrived at the station nearly half an hour before my train was due, and saw 'Schools' No 30918 *Hurstpierpoint* pass with the 8.45am Waterloo – Lymington Pier. In due course, the Weymouth train steamed into Platform 4, normally the Hampton Court platform, a 10-coach train hauled by BR Standard '5' 4-6-0 No 73089. The engine carried the Bournemouth line headcode discs, Nine Elms duty No 40, and a 70A shedplate. The coaches would have been stabled in the South Sidings at Wimbledon since the Friday afternoon, after working up to Waterloo as a Basingstoke train.

There was plenty of room when I got in, but the train was full by Eastleigh. We ran on the slow line as far as Worting Junction, calling at Woking, Farnborough and Basingstoke. Before passing Worting at 10.48, we were scheduled to be overtaken by four expresses from Waterloo: the 9.15 to Swanage; 9.24 to Weymouth; 9.35 to Bournemouth West and 9.42 to Lymington Pier. The 9.15, with 'Battle of Britain' Pacific No 34087 *145 Squadron*, went by at Surbiton, and the 9.24 and 9.35, both hauled by Standard '5' 4-6-0s, passed in the Woking area. The Lymington train was evidently running late and had to follow us all the way to Brockenhurst; in fact, No 30921 *Shrewsbury*

Below:
The train used on the journey described in the article, the summer Saturdays 9.24am Wimbledon–Weymouth, sets out from its starting point on 4 August 1962 behind BR '5' 4-6-0 No 73088 *Joyous Gard.* *S. Creer*

on the 9.42 drew up alongside at Southampton Central, 13 mins late, just as we were leaving.

That journey is memorable for some fascinating glimpses of steam working and of trains routed by lines nowadays disused or non-existent. At Walton-on-Thames carriage sidings, 'U1' 2-6-0 No 31907 was standing ready, with headboard 236 attached, to take the 10.5 empty stock to Waterloo, consisting of 10 coaches which would form the 10.54 departure for Swanage. As we pulled away from a signal at Byfleet Junction (we must have caught up the 8.59 am Waterloo to Alton stopping electric train), 'Q1' 0-6-0 No 33013 went round the curve towards Addlestone with a freight from Bevois Park, near Southampton, to Feltham marshalling yard.

While we were at Basingstoke, 'King Arthur' No 30782 *Sir Brian* departed at the head of the 10.35 semi-fast to Waterloo, made up to 10 coaches including restaurant car (as yet unstaffed) for the next working of the set, the 12.22 pm Waterloo – Bournemouth West. Standard '5' No 73085 then arrived on the 9.11 am Portsmouth Harbour – Wolverhampton Low Level, carrying the correct reporting number V87; this engine was to be relieved here, and its replacement, 'Modified Hall' No 6961 *Stedham Hall*, still carried reporting number 023 from its previous working. This revealed that it had reached Basingstoke in the small hours on the 10.55 pm Nottingham Victoria – Portsmouth. As we set off, Standard '4' 2-6-0 No 76013 clattered through on the 9 am Lymington Pier – Waterloo, non-stop from Winchester City, and 'Hall' No 6904 *Charfield Hall* could be seen on shed with reporting number 031 on its smokebox,

denoting its duty on the 6.05 am Birmingham Snow Hill – Bournemouth West.

Beyond Winchester we met the procession of Bournemouth line trains due in Waterloo at lunchtime, including two from Weymouth, one from Swanage and one from Lymington. These were followed by 'Battle of Britain' No 34054 *Lord Beaverbrook* with the 10.25 am Poole – Bradford Exchange, which would leave the Western Region at Banbury with another locomotive and head north up the former Great Central main line. The front three coaches of this train were labelled for Leicester Central.

As we drew into Brockenhurst it was clear that one of the celebrated Lymington engine changes was about to take place. Although slightly behind time, we waited there for four minutes. 'Q' 0-6-0 No

Left:
'Hall' 4-6-0 No 5986 *Arbury Hall* **has just taken over the 1.28pm Portsmouth Harbour—Birmingham Snow Hill from a BR '5' 4-6-0 at Basingstoke, and leaves for the Western Region, on 10 August 1963.**
S. A. Rocksborough Smith

Below left:
'King Arthur' 4-6-0 No 30782 *Sir Brian* **north of Winchester City on 16 July 1960 with the 6.22am Bournemouth Central—Woking.**   *L. Elsey*

Above:
The traditional water-stop at Southampton Central: the driver of a 'Battle of Britain' Pacific hastily pulls away the water hose. June 1965.
Roderick I.D. Hoyle

Below:
Winchester City on 3 May 1963, and 'Merchant Navy' 4-6-2 No 35011 *General Steam Navigation* **makes stately progress with the up 'Bournemouth Belle'. 'S15' 4-6-0 No 30498 is waiting to follow with a freight train.**   *Michael J. Fox*

30543 arrived in Platform 1, the up loop, with the 11.43 am Lymington Pier to Waterloo, and was uncoupled. The main line engine, 'Schools' No 30918 *Hurstpierpoint*, still carrying headboard 413 for the 8.45am ex-Waterloo, then approached from the direction of the turntable. The 'Schools' was too heavy for the Lymington branch, but short enough to be turned on the small turntable at Brockenhurst, and in 1961 there were duties for three Nine Elms members of the class to work to Brockenhurst and back on Saturdays with the Lymington boat trains.

Bournemouth shed had its usual array of locomotives, including 'King Arthur' No 30790 *Sir Villiars* and several Bulleid Pacifics. We reached Poole as another Standard '5', No 73021 of Bath Green Park shed, which had come down the Somerset & Dorset line with the 9.3 am from Bristol and would be terminating at Bournemouth West. In a siding at Poole stood No 34087 *145 Squadron*, which had overtaken us at Surbiton three hours earlier; this engine had been detached from the 9.15 Waterloo to Swanage at Wareham and was on its way to Bournemouth for turning and servicing before taking an afternoon train to London.

We had been stopped by signals four times on the way down, but the schedule was not exacting, and as I watched my train negotiate the sharp curve to Dorchester Junction box, it was two minutes early by the working book.

Coming back the following Saturday I faced a number of choices. Almost every train to London had some unusual feature. One express called at Surbiton and Wimbledon to set down only; on another I could have a non-stop run from

Bournemouth Central, if I paid the excess fare from Surbiton to Waterloo and back. There was even the 10.10 am from Weymouth, which stopped at every station as far as Woking except Redbridge, Millbrook, Swaythling and Shawford. But I selected the 11.23 am departure, the 11 am Weymouth – Waterloo, whose intermediate stops were at Wool, Wareham and Southampton Central. This was a five-coach train from Weymouth, and was attached at Wareham to the rear of the 11.34 from Swanage. The combined train then ran by way of 'Castleman's Snake,' otherwise known as the 'Old Road' from Hamworthy Junction to Lymington Junction through Wimborne and Ringwood, and avoiding Bournemouth.

BR Standard '4' 2-6-0 No 76058 came slowly round the curve and through Dorchester South station, stopped, and backed its train into the up platform. Two late-running Channel Islands boat trains from Waterloo, hauled by Bulleid Pacifics, passed the down platform in the space of five minutes. We reached Wareham at 11.47 am and it was fully 23 mins before we set off again. First, No 76058 was uncoupled, ran through the down platform and came on to the other end of the train. Nine minutes were to elapse before our next move because No 76015 was running late with the 11.12 am Bournemouth Central – Weymouth, and then No 76058 drew us on to the down line west of the station. We waited there for another five mins

before the main train from Swanage came in sight at Worgret Junction. No 34017 *Ilfracombe* was at the head of eight coaches, and carried Nine Elms duty No 30 and the Ringwood line headcode of three discs: one on each side of the smokebox door and one on the left side of the bufferbeam. While the Pacific took water, the Weymouth coaches were shunted to the back of its train and No 76058 was uncoupled. Until departure, the lengthy train fouled the crossover from the down line, and so the 9.15 am Waterloo – Swanage, which had by then approached behind No 34001 *Exeter*, could not obtain clearance into the down platform and was held on the far side of the level crossing. Meanwhile, yet another Pacific, No 34085 *501 Squadron,* had arrived tender-first five mins ahead of the 9.15, running light from Bournemouth, its home shed. This engine was now standing in the down bay platform by the water column, topping up for its next duty, which was to take over the 9.15 am from Waterloo for the rest of its journey and then haul the 1.23 pm Swanage – Waterloo throughout.

We were seven mins late leaving Wareham, and lost more time climbing from Hamworthy Junction to a brief meeting with the Somerset & Dorset line at Broadstone. From here to Lymington Junction, a distance of just under 22 miles, our schedule allowed 37 mins, probably because the 'West Country' class was (or certainly had been) officially restricted to 40 mph over the 'Old Road'. In fact No 34017 needed 30 mins only.

At Southampton Central, headboard 274 was tied to the smokebox of the Pacific, and after passing Eastleigh we overtook No 34094 *Mortehoe* on the slow line with the four coaches and two vans of the 10.10 from Weymouth. But the fable of the hare and

Below:
Carrying the route code for a train running via Ringwood, 'West Country' 4-6-2 No 34009 *Lyme Regis* **passes Millbrook on 16 July 1960 with the 10.54am Waterloo–Swanage** *R.A. Panting*

the tortoise came true on this occasion. After an unscheduled station stop at Woking, No 34017 shuddered to a halt outside Durnsford Road electric train depot and was unable to move any further. We stood there for 47 mins until 'Q1' No 33040 of Feltham shed came to our rescue, and after another 16 mins delay pulled the heavy train back into the platform at Wimbledon. Meanwhile six long-distance expresses had overtaken us on the up local line – the last of which was the 10.10 from Weymouth!

Above:
Dorchester South on 2 April 1967: having reversed into the up platform, BR '4' 2-6-0 No 76008 is ready to leave with a Weymouth–Bournemouth stopping train. *Ken Mould*

Below:
Shortly before withdrawal of the passenger service from Bournemouth–Ringwood–Brockenhurst, 'U' 2-6-0 No 31632 with the 1.30pm Bournemouth–Brockenhurst passes BR '5' 4-6-0 No 73041 on a Weymouth–Bournemouth train at Poole. 9 February 1964. *A.W. Smith*

Tickets
Michael Farr

THOMAS EDMONDSON (1792-1851) pioneered the card ticket system used worldwide which carries his name to this day.

Born in Lancaster, his practical abilities led him to an apprenticeship with the furniture firm of Gillow's, where he made his mark. From there he went into a cabinet-making partnership at Carlisle, but the business closed.

Edmondson found employment with the Newcastle and Carlisle Railway at Milton station, later renamed Brampton Junction, and now, unstaffed, known as Brampton. The inspiration for his ticket system is reputed to have come to him 'in a flash' as he walked near Talkin Tarn, near Milton, and, at first, he used his handwritten tickets at the station.

The N&CR was slow to accept his system, but the manager of the Leeds and Manchester Railway

tempted him away with an offer of an enhanced salary and the opportunity to develop the tickets and equipment for sale internationally at a royalty of 10/- (50p) per route mile.

The firm of John B. Edmondson (Thomas' son) listed in its catalogue machines for printing and dating tickets, racks, cupboards and drawers for storing them, clippers for marking and cancelling the cards and, finally, a machine to shred the used tickets to prevent misuse!

The machines still used by BR at Crewe to print card tickets share several features with Edmondson's own designs, and many British Rail stations retain their counter-mounted dating press with oval brass plate inscribed 'Edmondson's Patent'.

The year 1986 sees the 150th anniversary of Edmondson's card railway tickets; by then the majority of British Rail's passengers are likely to be travelling with tickets of the computer age, with most journeys outside the conurbations begun and completed at Open Stations and with ticket checking carried out on the train.

Already British Rail is evaluating the latest generation of station ticket issuing machines, the APTIS – All-Purpose Ticket Issuing System – developed in association with Thorn-EMI.

This equipment, producing a credit-card sized ticket (one for single journeys; two separate cards for returns), is now experimentally installed at certain selected stations and will form the greater part of a £30 million project to modernise fare collection, with computerised fares store, data retrieval and accountancy.

THOMAS EDMONDSON,
An Old Lancastrian.
1792—1851.

Left:
Thomas Edmondson, transport ticket pioneer. Born 30 June 1792, died 22 June 1851.
Science Museum/Crown Copyright.

Right:
A main line station ticket office, believed to be Leicester, when the Edmondson system was generally used. Note the low benches so that staff of short stature could reach the top rows in the racks.

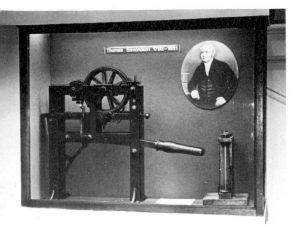

The B100 model machine is capable of carrying up to 80 destinatons. Trials with other types of self-service (POTIS) machines are to be conducted at Welwyn Garden City and Pontypridd.

Concurrent with these developments in ticket issue, the checking and collecting of tickets is being brought into line with European practice. Already, in much of Scotland and the West Country, station entrances are unmanned, giving passengers free access and exit. Tickets are checked regularly on the train, and for passengers joining at unstaffed stations, fares are collected en route.

On Paytrains, a compact portable version of the machine (PORTIS) will produce a passenger ticket with all the details clearly printed – an improvement on the slips of often indecipherable paper produced from the bus-type machines widely used today by conductor-guards. PORTIS equipment has been tested on the Bristol-Severn Beach branch, the Reading-Tonbridge service and in the Leeds and Newcastle areas.

BR also sees a need for a third type of fare collection – a passenger-operated self-service machine. One such, marketed in the UK by Agiticket Ltd, which has seen trials at Charing Cross, offers a choice of 40 destinations and accepts six different coins, or £5 notes, and gives change.

It's the passenger's duty to see that he has a valid ticket before setting out on a journey from a staffed station. People who avoid buying a ticket when they could do so face paying full fare – and a little more in the form of a penalty.

Some passengers are naturally irritated at having to show their tickets frequently, but inspectors are surprisingly effective at remembering the tickets they have already checked – even, as the writer recalls, when covering a full-length journey by IC125 unit to Penzance.

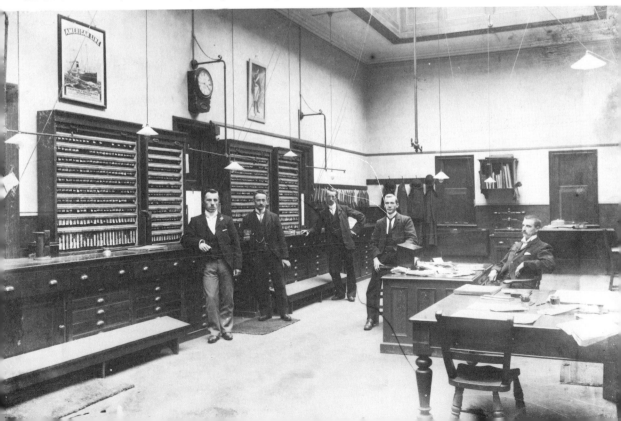

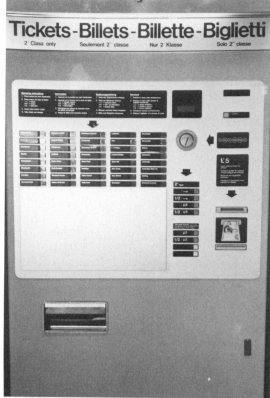

PORTIS equipment:

Top:

The prototype machine for on-train use. Production models are expected to be more compact. Tickets produced by these machines contain more information than current Paytrain equipment. *BR*

Above right:

Agiticket Ltd PORTIS machine, on trial at Charing Cross station, London. *Lee Gray, Agiticket Ltd*

Above:

Prototype APTIS machine on trial at various BR stations. This produces tickets on blank cards of credit card size: one ticket for singles, two cards for returns. *Thorn-EMI Electronics Ltd*

In surburban areas, and particularly in London, ticket checking at stations is likely to remain. Certainly, the barriers planned for ARC (Automatic Revenue Control) are now seen to be 'not user-friendly'. In any case, a barrier designed to permit the ingress of a passenger struggling with heavy luggage is hardly a deterrent to an agile youngster.

Even though their country cousins may pass freely on and off station platforms, the city dweller can continue to expect checks at stations, although

even these may be carried out randomly and more will be done on trains.

Historically, Edmondson devised his ticket system to meet three criteria:

(1) A receipt for the passenger for the fare he has paid.
(2) A check on the ticket office staff to ensure that all money paid goes to the railway.
(3) Advice to staff en route of how far, and by what route, the passenger may travel for the fare paid.

Edmondson's neat card tickets, size $2\frac{1}{4}$ in by $1\,{}^3/_{16}$ in, with dating presses, racks, printing machines, clippers and the machine for destroying used tickets, were adopted by railway companies at home and abroad throughout the Victorian era.

When in 1912 the GWR installed AEG Regina machines (a German design) at Snow Hill station, Birmingham, the tickets were printed on blank card as they were issued. Accountancy was simplified by using a built-in totaliser, there was no risk of printed tickets being stolen en route from the printers and no need to hold vast stocks of individually printed tickets for every journey made regularly. Even with this mechanisation, Edmondson-size ticket blanks were issued.

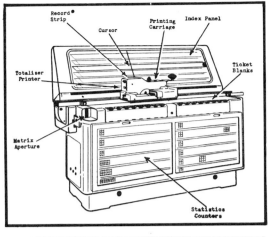

Record Strip · Cursor · Printing Carriage · Index Panel · Ticket Blanks · Totaliser Printer · Matrix Aperture · Statistics Counters

No doubt World War 1 and its aftermath discouraged British railways from planning large installations of German machines, and it was not until the mid-1920s that Snow Hill received further Regina equipment.

Heavy traffic on suburban lines encouraged the use of Rapidprinters, marketed in the UK by Westinghouse and used extensively by London Transport ticket offices. Various self-service, coin-operated machines were installed, some being adapted from the chocolate bar vending machines and requiring tickets two or three times thicker than normal.

But, apart from isolated mechanisation (including the Bellgraphic manuscript tickets), the Edmondson system remained in use until Nationalisation.

In the 1950s, British Railways began a programme of modernising ticket offices. Pigeon-hole windows gave way to plate glass and Multiprinter machines, developed from the Regina and supplied by Westinghouse, appeared at major stations. Another model, the Flexiprinter, was provided for use at suburban stations where large quantities of tickets to a limited number of destinations could be rapidly produced. The installation at Cardiff General to serve the 'Valleys' services was the largest in Europe.

Above left:
The Westinghouse/AEG Flexiprinter machine is designed for rapid production of a limited range of ticket types. It can handle season tickets, as well as standard Edmondson-type cards. *BR*

Top:
Outline sketch of the Westinghouse/AEG Multiprinter. *BR*

Above:
Bellmatic ticket cabinets enable the whole printed area of the ticket to be on view. Tickets are removed from the top of each pile – the reverse of the traditional gravity feed rack. Also illustrated are Ultimatic machines dispensing pre-printed paper tickets.
Bell Punch Co/Control Systems Ltd.

Rapidprinters were used for the most popular issues at busy stations, while the Handiprinter (another Westinghouse product) produced a yellow paper ticket. The Bell Punch/Control Systems Ultimatic machines, issuing pre-printed paper tickets, are still used extensively, 30 years after their introduction. Leeds had a sizeable installation before the extension of Paytrain operations.

Above:
NCR cash registers in use at Horsham station. The clerk inserts the ticket, records the passenger's fare and the date and amount are automatically printed on the ticket. *BR*

Above right:
A ticket as used with the NCR system on the Southern Region. *BR*

Right:
The Glasgow–Wemyss Bay/Gourock services were chosen for an experiment in revenue control with magnetic coded tickets and automatic barriers (seen here at Glasgow Central). *BR*

The Southern Region, with particularly heavy commuter traffic, was largely bypassed by the 'machine era' of the 1950s. A major problem with issuing ordinary single and return tickets is that by law they must carry the current fare. As prices increased, so the fares on old stocks had to be altered by hand or, in the case of the Multi and Flexiprinter machines, by changing the printing plates and pins which actuated the totaliser.

The SR's chosen solution used a machine like a cash register to overprint the fare and date upon issue. At the same time, the takings of a particular shift could be recorded by pressing a single button, so speeding the changeover of staff. Separate, printed ticket stocks of Edmondson-size tickets were still required for all normal journeys, the vertical design incorporating boxes or spaces to accommodate the machine-printed details, including the machine's serial number. The ticket serial numbers were pre-printed at the *top* of the cards to permit the use of spring-loaded Bellmatic racks, so that the top ticket would be visible.

These NCR21 machines were first installed at East Croydon, and from 1966 spread to almost all the SR's stations, until a total of over 800 machines had been deployed. The later models (NCR24) were designed to print over £1,000 when long-distance annual season tickets ran into four-figure fares, and the NCR21 models were adapted later.

The principle of pricing tickets on issue was a clear success and three other BR Regions – Western, Scottish and Eastern – adopted the NCR51 machine. In this case, additional information (station destinaton code, ticket type and station of issue) could be overprinted, enabling a standard stock of semi-blank tickets to be used all over the country. As the tickets are of no use until validated on the machine, they present no security risk in transit or in store, and printing can be entrusted to commercial companies.

A similar system using Hugin machines was tested at selected stations but was not developed, although some of the machines were disposed of cheaply and are now used by independent lines.

The Glasgow – Wemyss Bay and Gourock services were chosen for an experiment in revenue control with magnetic coded tickets and automatic barriers. The stored journey system was used, with one or two journey tickets available in either direction, instead of singles or returns Seasons were replaced with multiple journey tickets (up to 50) and an indicator on the barrier showed how many 'lives' were left on a ticket.

Glasgow was also the venue for trials of the Westinghouse Small Stations Ticket Issuing System (SSTIS), producing a single credit-card size ticket for single or return journeys. From this was developed the Intermediate Ticket Issuing System (INTIS), both types requiring blanks pre-printed with the destination station, as with the NCR51.

An advantage with the APTIS, the latest generation of station ticket issuing machines, is that starting and destination stations alike are printed by the issuing machine, whose memory can recall all fares listed in the BR Selective Prices Manual, as well as specially programmed prices. Up to 24 of the most common destinations can be selected by using a single button on the keyboard. The rest of as many as 2,500 destinations can be accessed by keying in the first four letters of the destination, allowing for 'Llan. . .', 'South. . .', 'North. . .', etc.

Initial trials of the APTIS promise well for its introduction throughout the BR system. Until now, the UK has tended to lag behind other European rail networks when it comes to ticket issue and collection, but it seems likely that BR will eventually have by far the most economical national fare collection system for self-service, ticket office, or on-train use. In short, it is fitting for the country which pioneered the Edmondson card system in the year that Queen Victoria came to the throne.

Above:
Ticket queue at London Victoria station.
J.G. Glover

Left:
When the Travel Centre was opened at Edinburgh Waverley in 1970, Hugin machines were installed, validating pre-printed tickets on issue. *BR*

85

Requiem for Reddish TMD
David Rose

MONDAY, 16 May 1983 will go down as the day another traction depot was closed on British Rail. For some people, it was the end of an era. I first came to know Reddish depot in 1965 as the archetypal schoolboy who wanted to watch trains go by.

Reddish Traction Maintenance Depot, as it was known in its latter years, may be seen in retrospect as a outpost on a branch line from nowhere to nowhere. In its earlier years, however, it represented the golden future for British Railways.

The section of line on which the depot was located runs from Chorlton Junction, through Wilbraham Road, Fallowfield, Levenshulme, Hyde Road (Gorton) to a triangle of junctions at Gorton and Openshaw and Fairfield stations. From Chorlton Junction to Fallowfield was opened by the Manchester Sheffield and Lincolnshire Railway on 1 October 1891, and the second section, from Fallowfield to Gorton and Fairfield, on 2 May 1892. This line was used by services from the Cheshire Lines Committee territory and Manchester's impressive Central station to Guide Bridge and further afield over the Pennines.

With the approach of the electrification of the Woodhead route at 1,500V dc overhead, the building of Reddish depot started late in 1952. It had a two-bay, four-road layout, two roads having electric overhead wires and inspection pits for testing electric stock and the other roads seved the repair bay. The bay was equipped with the customary facilities, such as an overhead gantry crane and a tyre profiling lathe, to enable any repair, large or small, to be carried out on the depot's fleet of 1,500V dc Bo-Bo and Co-Co locomotives and also the three-car electric multiple-unit sets for the Glossop services.

This made Reddish the first depot to be purpose-built for main line electric locomotives. Another

claim to fame for Reddish was that the 'Midland Pullman' diesel multiple-unit sets, effectively the forerunners of the InterCity 125 sets, were serviced there. Evidence of this could still be found on the outside walls where stencilled notices read 'Pullman oil' and 'Sulzer oil'. I came to know the depot in 1965. My enthusiast friend and I had always lived in Reddish, and from my bedroom window I could look across the fields and see the depot in the distance. We started to visit the depot on Saturday mornings. First, we wandered around the depot perimeter fence 'copping' the locomotives outside, and then going across the ponds to spend two hours trainspotting at the place where the line crosses the Hope Valley route. Then, it was a case of watch the four directions for a trace of steam and keep your eyes on the signals. It was 12 months later before the two of us plucked up courage to ask if we could look inside the depot.

That first day, two small boys appeared at the foreman's office door and expected to be thrown off the premises. We were surprised to be told: 'Yes, you can look round. Watch what you are doing and don't climb on the engines!' This was followed by,

Right:
Inscription on the cab side of Class 76 electric locomotive No 76.037 at Reddish TMD, 24 March 1983. *Alec Jones*

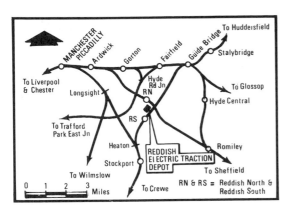

'Report back here before you leave.' We were delighted. Inside at last! We could add 20 numbers to the day's list. After that, Saturday wasn't Saturday without a visit to Reddish. In those days, the locomotives on shed and the traffic that passed were equally varied. On shed would be numerous Bo-Bo electric locomotives, numbered 26000 in those days; six or so what were to become Class 40s; a couple of Class 25s; some of the dc electric multiple-units and a Pullman diesel set.

Occasionally, Reddish would have a rare visitor. The Metrovick Co-Bo diesel locomotives paid the odd visit, sometimes a 'Peak', a Class 47 diesel locomotive, or a diesel multiple-unit formation. After an inspection inside, we set off to our vantage point for the rest of the morning.

At 10.20 every Saturday, a Manchester-bound train on the Hope Valley line would produce a 'Peak'. The Marple and New Mills services were in the hands of various types of diesel multiple unit. It was not unusual for a dmu formation to go off Reddish shed after repair in the morning and then appear on the Hope Valley line before lunch.

Freight trains were frequent on both lines and were in the hands of 'Black 5s', Stanier '8F' 2-8-0s, BR '9F' 2-10-0s, and occasionally something special would materialise. The first 'Jubilee' I saw, No 45647 *Sturdee*, was heading a freight train towards Guide Bridge. 'WD' 2-8-0s passed by on a couple of occasions, and my one and only sighting of a former Crosti-boilered 2-10-0 was of No 92020, also on a freight working.

With weekly visits to Reddish it didn't take long to see all seven 'EM2' class Co-Co electric locomotives, but the 'EM1' Bo-Bos were a different matter. Some were stabled at Guide Bridge, and others were overhauled at Doncaster Works, but some members of the class were conspicuous by their absence at Reddish. My 'bogie' happened to be No 26014. This locomotive was the last one I needed to complete my 'set' of the class. Our regular visits failed to produce this elusive 'EM1'. One sortie to Guide Bridge only succeeded in our being sent away without a single number. It was always a well-guarded stabling point!

At least six months passed before No 26014 spent a Saturday on Reddish depot. What a relief that day was! We were beginning to give up hope.

9 September 1973 proved to be a memorable day for BR had arranged an Open Day at Reddish depot. On display were examples of Classes 47, 40, 25, Class 87 No 87.001 and air-conditioned Mark 2D passenger coaches. Various items of rolling stock and freight wagons were on show, along with the Longsight breakdown crane. Steam was also in

Below:
Reddish depot, with the Hyde Road Junction–Trafford Park E. Junction line in the foreground, 5 March 1983.   *W. Sartori*

evidence as 'Jubilee' No 5596 *Bahamas* from the Dinting Railway Centre offered footplate rides for the day.

But what of the later years? By the middle/late 1970s, my visits to Reddish had dwindled to once every three months. By then the Class 76s were fitted for multiple-working of coal trains over Woodhead. Some had been spruced up and looked very smart, although the number of serviceable examples was beginning to decline. Also, the wheel lathe was attracting a wider range of locomotives and rolling stock. Class 304 and 310 25kV ac electric multiple-units appeared for tyre turning, generally towed to Reddish by a Class 40. Some of the Class 87s spent time at Reddish for modifications. The average number of Class 40s on depot might be as many as 10 or 12. The occasional Bury third-rail dc electric multiple-unit arrived for attention. On one Saturday, a Wirral and a Mersey dc emu set were at Reddish awaiting attention. Six Class 24 diesel locomotives spent several months in store at Reddish before final withdrawal, and on most Sundays all eight electric units from the Glossop services could be seen.

Of the diesel locomotives, Classes 37s, 'Peaks', 47s, and 31s recently became regular visitors, and until the demise of the depot Class 25s became almost as numerous as '40s'. Wagons and carriages also filled more of the depot's maintenance capacity and, for a short period, a car-carrying wagon set took up the full length of one inside road. Then came the abandonment of the Woodhead route electrification.

With the decision to sell the Class 76s for scrap, the writing was on the wall for Reddish depot as its allocation was removed. The closure date was originally fixed for March 1983, but the deadline was extended to 16 May.

Reddish depot:

Above:
View looking north of the maintenance bay. Pantographs for electric multiple-units stand left foreground.

Below:
Looking at the depot from the north end exit roads showing the diesel fuel storage tanks. The lorries are waiting to remove material from the doomed depot. *Both: David Rose*

With the date set, the depot was slowly cleared of stock. Its Class 76s were photographed in rakes being towed to various scrapyards. Diesel work was suspended and transferred elsewhere. The last diesel locomotive on Reddish was No 25.294 and it was towed away as a condemned locomotive on Tuesday, 10 May. By Sunday, 15 May, all that was left was a small complement of staff filling a line of BR lorries with spares and equipment. There were also seven Class 76s: Nos 76.043, 76.052, 76.055, 76.004, 76.002, 76.048 and 76.050.

These locomotives were awaiting the return of bearings and parts from the scrapyards where their compatriots had gone. This was to enable the safe removal by rail of these last seven electric locomotives.

The rest of the depot spoke of emptiness and dereliction. The last Class 504 multiple-units left for service on 14 May. The others were towed to Guide Bridge for servicing and storage. It was surprising just how many enthusiasts came to Reddish that last Sunday to pay their last respects. The departure board at the depot said it all: 'We have run out of puffers.'

Motive power on Reddish depot:

Above right:
Class 40 No 40.168. Note the old number, 368, applied at one end. *Alan Sherratt*

Right:
The board says it all inside the depot. The times are those for the Class 506 electric multiple-units due off shed to cover Saturday services on 14 May 1983. *David Rose*

Below:
The line-up of the last Class 76 electric locomotives inside the depot on 15 May 1983. *David Rose*

The 'Y' of it all

Eric Ellis

IMAGINE a spring afternoon in 1952, and a sunny spot on a grassy embankment near Crewe. A hooter blows; then, with a rush and roar, a brand-new four-cylinder *Compound* freight locomotive passes hauling coal wagons. I can already hear the disbelievers; incredible, and incorrect they would say. They would be wrong. I am writing of course, of Crewe, Virginia, USA: on the Norfolk and Western Railway, and its compound articulated 2-8-8-2s, the 'Y6bs'

British enthusiasts, and particularly those of the LMS genre brought up on the legend of F.W. Webb, may find it difficult to believe that one US railroad, against all trends in its own country, continued to build a successful series of compound locomotives that began with a basic design in 1910, contined through five further classes, was last built in 1952, and in that same year at worst equalled, and probably bested, a brace of brand-new diesels in road tests.

Compound Mallets had been introduced by the Baltimore & Ohio Railroad in 1904, and over the next 15/20 years many hundreds were placed in service by a number of railroads. They eliminated double heading in the era of 'drag' freights (long, slow trains) and also were used extensively in banking (pushing).

More modern practice in the 1930s was to build non-compound articulateds, with larger driving wheels, for higher speeds. The N&W had them – the 'A' 2-6-6-4s – but for certain types of work such as mine runs, pusher service and freights in hilly country, the railroad stuck to the old formula.

Now for another surprise. The N&W's first 2-8-8-2 compounds were a failure. Five 'Y1' locomotives were delivered by Baldwin in 1910, numbered 995-99. They had 75 sq ft grate area, 24½in/39in x 30in cylinders, 56in driving wheels, Walschaerts valve gear, piston valves on both cylinders. 200lb boiler pressure, Alligator crossheads, a 14 ton, 9,000 gallon capacity tender and a tractive effort of 66,900lbs. They were not superheated, but had the front section of the boiler barrel as a separate feed-water heater, with an ash chamber between it and the boiler proper. This arrangement proved to be their undoing, geting clogged up with ash very easily. Interestingly, a reheater was fitted for the expended high-pressure steam before it entered the low-pressure cylinders.

One was tested against a Chesapeake & Ohio RR 2-6-6-2 which bested it, and resulted in the (successful) introduction of the N&W's own 'Z1' 2-6-6-2s, built between 1912 and 1918, and numbering some 400 locomotives

A gap of eight years, and the desire for more power, resulted in the Roanoke-designed 'Y2' of 1918. No 1700 of this type had a longer cylinder stroke, 32in, 96 sq ft of grate area, 240 lbs boiler pressure, Baker valve gear, different to the 'Y1' and a more conventional boiler barrel. At this point, the United States Railroad Administration took over the administration of all US railroads, and designed standard locomotives which it more or less directed to whoever needed them. The USRA used the 'Y2' as its basic 2-8-8-2 design and allowed the N&W to build more for itself (Nos 1701-10) and also ordered from Baldwin (Nos 1711-30). Some were finished later than the 'Y3' class, and were known as 'Y2a' (Nos 1705-10) and incorporated minor improvements derived from the 'Y3s'. Five were fitted with tender boosters in the 1930s, and most had their boiler pressure increased to 270lbs in the 1940s. They had smokebox hung air-compressors, which made them uglier than most. Fifteen were sold to the Denver & Rio Grande Western RR, during World War 2, with two acquired by the Utah Copper Company. All were scrapped by 1951.

The 'Y3s' were the USRA-designed 2-8-8-2s. The first five (Nos 2000-2004) were built at Alco's Schenectady works, and were intended for the Virginian Railway, having actually been numbered (900-04) and lettered so, before being diverted to the N&W. They had 57in driving wheels and a 25in diameter hp cylinder, with air-pumps on the front end, and were delivered in 1919. Nos 2005-49 were also built in 1919, by Alco and Baldwin, with 16 ton/12,000 gallon tenders, In 1923, Richmond supplied Nos 2050-79, classed 'Y3a' with 20 ton/ 15,000 gallon tenders. They were long-lived engines, being upgraded with Worthington BL feedwater heaters (on the side of the boiler) in the 1930s, with the air compressors moved to the opposite side for balance. In the 1940s their boiler pressure was increased to 270lbs, and many of this series received the older bar frames and cylinders

when the 'Y5' class was rebuilt with cast engine beds. Eight were coupled to secondhand tenders of 26 tons/22,000 gallons in the 1950s and 19 sold, (six to the Pennsylvania RR, eight to the Santa Fe, then Virginian and five to the Union Pacific) in World War 2. The last was withdrawn in 1958.

The 'Y4s' (originally 'Y3b') were really 'Y3a' with minor improvements. Nos 2080-89 were built at Richmond in 1927. again, the boiler pressure as built was 240lbs and became 270lbs in the 1940s. The driving wheels were increased from 57in to 58in. Their smokebox doors were originally round, with a flat bottom, but these were changed to a fully round one. Problems were experienced with the massive piston thrusts which resulted in frame-twisting, but these were overcome. Some secondhand 27t/24,000 gal tenders riding on four-wheel trucks were paired to all ten of the class in 1953. All were withdrawn in 1958.

After 1927, the N&W did not purchase any new conventional steam locomotives from private builders and the 'Y5s' were all built at Roanoke between 1930 and 1932, Nos 2090-2119. The most important improvement on the previous class was the redesigned steam and exhaust passages, resulting in a massive 'bridge' of pipework below the smokebox. This, in addition to increasing the 14in diameter valves to 18in, and the increase in grate area to 106sq ft, with an initial 280lbs boiler pressure (changed to 300 lbs at building) resulted in a more powerful, free-steaming locomotive. Tenders were on six-wheeled trucks and were of 26 tons /22,000 gallons capacity with a cast-steel frame for the first time. Some had front-end throttles, instead of being

Below:
'Y5' 2-8-8-2 No 2092, built at the Norfolk & Western Railway's Roanoke shops. Note the 'bridge' of pipework beneath the smokebox. This was the engine wrecked in a derailment in 1937.
Norfolk & Western Railway

positioned in the dome. They had a tractive effort (simple) of 152,206 lbs and 126,838 lbs (compound).

All the class were upgraded in the 1940s with cast steel engine beds, roller bearings on all axles, and firebox lagging below the running boards (unusual in American practice). To this specification, they were considered the virtual equivalent of the 'Y6' class. One was wrecked in a derailment which caused a boiler explosion in 1937 (No 2092), and another boiler explosion in 1950 meant a new boiler for No 2114. It had been caused by a suction hose collapsing, because it had not been replaced at a recent overhaul, with consequent loss of feed-water.

The 'Y6s', Nos 2120-54 built by Roanoke between 1936-40, were also a similar follow-on to the previous class with a redesigned blastpipe giving the chimney a 'leant-forward' look and had front-end throttles. They also had outside bearing leading and trailing trucks for the first time, and the later ones, needle roller bearings in the motion. 'Y6as' Nos 2155-70 – Roanoke 1942, had slightly different feed-water heaters, covered sandpipes, and some had a significant change in that a longer combustion chamber was incorporated, reducing tube length from 24ft to 20ft, so increasing combustion efficiency. The 'Y6bs' Nos 2171-2200 were built from 1948-1952, partly to offset the removal of electric traction through the Elkhorn Tunnel. These comprised the final class of the 2-8-8-2 compounds. Again, the process of improvement continued with larger exhaust passages and a change of feed-water heater, now mounted on the smokebox. The fronts were different, too, as an oblong door, hinged at the

Blue Ridge, Virginia in September 1957. 'A' class
Mallet No 1219 storms through.   *J.N. Westwood*

bottom, was installed initially on an extended smokebox with a flat bottom, to the first fifteen to be built. With the relocation of the hot-water feed-pump to the side of the smokebox from underneath, these were altered to be the same as the later members of the class. Typical dimensions of the 'Y6b' were as follows: height 15ft 9¾in; length overall 114ft 10½in; boiler barrel tapering from 8ft 8in to 8ft 1in; firebox 8ft 10in x 14ft 2in; boiler pressure 300lbs. Baker valve gear; 25in/39in x 32in cylinders; 4ft 10in diameter driving wheels, 2ft 6in truck wheels. The grate area 106 sq ft; heating surface, 4,915 sq ft; superheater 1,478 sq ft; tractive effort (simple), 152,206 lbs; (compound), 126,838lbs. The axle loading was 29 tons approx. The tenders had capacity for 30 tons of coal and 22,000 gallons of water.

The compounding control system was also altered, and parts relocated for easier maintenance. There were three ways of admitting steam to the cylinders: simple – both hp and lp cylinders receiving live steam, and exhausting directly to atmosphere; compound – live steam to hp cylinders, exhausting through an intercepting valve/receiver to the lp cylinders, thence to atmosphere; compound with 'booster' steam – as compound, but with some live steam introduced through the intercepting valve to the lp cylinders. Typical operation might be to start a heavy train in the simple mode, go over to compound as soon as moving reasonably well, and then using booster

steam for any stiff gradients where the extra power would be useful. These modifications were the last to be applied to all modern 2-8-8-2s in 1953-55, and so increased the power from the leading engine unit that slipping presented a considerable problem. Fourteen tons of lead poured into the bed casting of all 'Y5', 'Y6' and 'Y6a' front engines to cure the problem, and the process of continual improvement and development begun in 1918 came to an end. 1955 was the year that the first road switcher diesel-electrics appeared on the N&W Railway.

Three years earlier, the company had decided to test an 'A' and a 'Y6b' against diesel traction. General Motors supplied a 6,000 hp four-unit diesel electric locomotive, and it was pitted against 'A' No 1239 and 'Y6b' No 2197, over flat and hilly terrain alike. In the end, it was just about a draw. The diesel units were better at starting and at low speeds, were bested in power output by the 'Y6b' between 18 and 36mph and showed to advantage thereafter, although not superior to the 'A'. The fuel costs per ton-mile were slightly in the diesels' favour. Steam was better at working heavy trains without stops. It is said that the General Motors engineers had to uprate their diesel engines by 200 hp to try to get the edge on the steamers.

Another innovation of the 1950s was the use of auxiliary tenders, 'canteens' as they were known. Of 16 tons/20,000 gallon capacity, they cut out many water-stops, on a railway that did not use water troughs, and where the starting of a 10,000 ton coal

train was expensive in terms of fuel and water consumed.

'Y' class locomotives were used all over the N&W system on everything from switching, hump duties, pushing, low-speed coal trains, mixed freights and mine runs. They could be seen from Norfolk to Columbus, Hagerstown to Bristol, and, as each new version came out for main line work, so the older types would be put out to grass on branch line and secondary work until eventually retired. In 1955, those on duty with coal trains through the mountains were averaging 6,000 miles a month – not bad at all when one looks elsewhere.

Probably the best known duties were lifting 13,000 (U.S.) ton coal trains out of Roanoke, and eastwards over Blue Ridge (ruling gradient of 1 in 83) in the 1950s. The sight of a 'Y6' with canteen leading an 'A' with a canteen, followed by miles of clanking coal hoppers, with a 'Y6' pushing at the rear, all 'down on their knees' as they crawled up the grade must have been one of the most stirring sights in railroading anywhere. The noise, interspersed with crossing calls from the engines' hooters, would have sent shivers down anyone's spine.

And that might not have been the end of it. In 1936, a proposed 'Y7' was put forward. This was to have been a simple expansion loco with 26in x 30in cylinders. 9ft 4in diameter boiler, 130 sq ft grate area with 5ft 3in driving wheels and 153,000lbs tractive effort. Presumably for freight use on the flatter parts of the system, such a machine would have been able to raise train speeds. A proposed US Federal law to limit the length of trains to 70 cars, which was never enacted, in addition to the improvements to the existing compound 'Ys' put paid to the scheme.

The 'Y' series of locomotives finished their time away from the main line, the last one in steam being No 2190 at Williamson on 6 May 1960. Although there were plans to save some of the class for emergencies, the policy of Stuart Saunders (who became president in 1955 and was a lawyer) was to scrap the lot. Two escaped; 'Y4' No 2050 is preserved at Union, Illinois and 'Y6a' No 2156 at the National Museum of Transport, St Louis, Missouri.

Sounds and film of those giants at work exist, chiefly of Blue Ridge coal trains. These are very impressive, but I also like the short sequence on one record of a 'Y6' leaving Waynesboro' on the Shenodoah Valley line, first working as a simple, then changing over to compound. It sums up the design philosophy of the locomotives admirably.

Sources:
1. *N and W: Giant of Steam* – L.I. Jeffries – Pruett Publishing Co, Pueblo, Colorado.
2. Arthur M. Bixby Snr – Curator, Roanoke Transportation Museum, Roanoke, Virginia.

Five railway houses

Dorothy Cowlin

IN AN area of North Yorkshire nowadays known officially as Ryedale, there once ran a branch of the North Eastern Railway from Pilmoor, on the York-Darlington main line, to the market town of Malton. From a junction at Gilling, another branch ran through Pickering and a series of small country stations in the Vale of Pickering, to Seamer, outside Scarborough. The Gilling-Malton section opened in May 1853, Gilling-Pickering by 1875, and Pickering-Seamer in May 1882, against considerable local opposition. Gilling-Malton and Seamer-Pickering were closed for all traffic in 1964.

Although both lines are now only a grass-grown memory, many of the station houses and out-buildings still stand. They were solidly built, most of them in stone, with a certain stylishness, but with something that stamps them immediately as 'railway houses'.

In earlier days, the smallest country station had its own station-master, and the railway provided each with a house, often attached to the station offices and waiting-rooms for passengers. Decent, even stylish, they were not provided with what would be considered essential amenities today. The houses were without bathrooms, and bereft of electricity and gas. A few had WCs, if only for the benefit of passengers. One of the perks of a country station-master was the sale of coal from railway bunkers, supplied by rail to the station yard. Nowadays, the coal travels by road, but sometimes is still retailed from the old bunkers in the goods yard.

When the branch lines were closed, many of the station houses were offered at less than market price to the redundant station-master, or some other employee. And, even in 1964, although still unprovided with 'mod-cons', some employees accepted the offer.

One such was Frederick Wright, in charge of Slingsby station, on the Gilling-Malton section. He bought not only the house, but the land attached, with its sidings and sheds. He proceeded to convert the house, inside and out, into as elegant a country residence as anyone could wish. He installed big, new picture-windows, one of them a fine bow. What had been the Ladies Waiting Room was converted into a sun-lounge, with a quarter circle of glass. From the south the house is completely transformed, but from the north, where it once looked out on to the track, it is still easily recognisable as a railway house. The platform flag-stones remain, although the intervening trackbed is filled up to their level.

Later, the land where the sidings and goods shed once stood was sold to a caravan club. Well-drained and firm for its original purpose, it was admirably suited for its new role. Nowadays grassed over, with the goods shed demolished (although its only too solid floor remains) and with a screen of trees, the small, stone weigh-house (now a store for the club) alone betrays the railway origins of the site.

The next station north west of Slingsby was Hovingham Spa, seat of the Worsley family. When the railway came in 1853 it was hoped that it would promote the development of a spa in the vicinity, which accounted for the name of the station. The medicinal waters gushed forth about 1½ miles away, where a handsome bath house was built for the patients. In the village, an equally handsome hotel, the Worsley Arms, was erected for their accommodation.

Both buildings still stand. The bath house is now a private residence and the Worsley Arms remains a hotel. But by the middle of the 19th century the medicinal waters alone were not enough. Patients also required entertainment, more readily available at older spa towns like Scarborough and Harrogate. Hovingham Spa never really made its mark. In view of its history, it seems entirely fitting that Hovingham station house should find fresh employment as a medical centre, but not immediately after sale by BR. At the time of closure, it was bought by the sitting tenant, Mr Hartley, who put in basic amenities, and made minor alterations to the station house's structure. It was not until 1975 that Dr Cunningham and his wife saw the possibilities of the location, and bought the house and its surrounding land.

At Hovingham, neither of the two goods sheds had been demolished. One of them now serves as the medical centre itself, comprising a consulting-

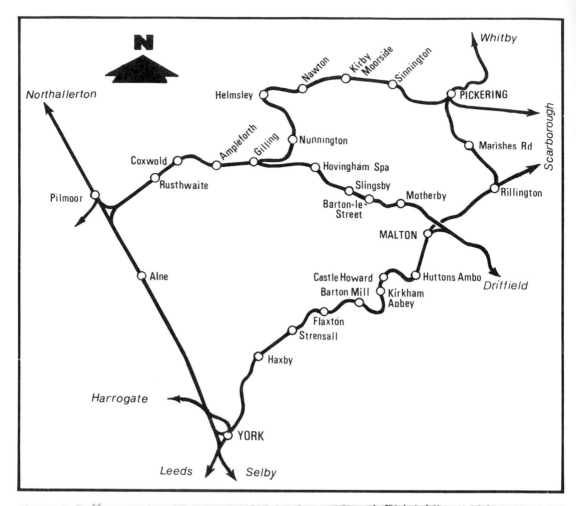

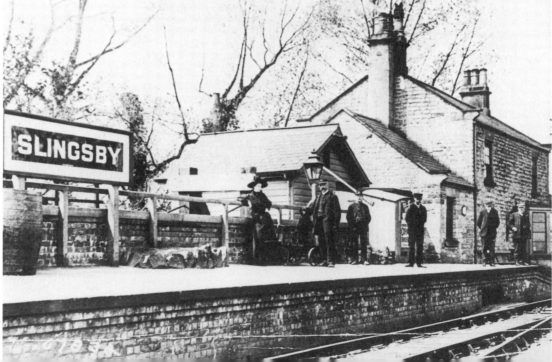

room, reception and waiting-rooms, and a store for medicines. The large arched entrances, where once goods wagons entered, have been glassed-in, to provide surprisingly classical-looking windows.

Hovingham's station house, now the doctor's home, rather unusually in this area is brick-built, but just as stylish as those constructed of stone. Most of the alterations have been to the interior and have involved knocking two rooms into one, and similar replanning. In this way, what were once booking-office and waiting-room have been combined to provide a fine, well-proportioned drawing-room, with ample space for a grand piano. There are windows on three sides, those at the back looking out on the trackbed and platform, and the latter has been retained. It runs the whole length of the house and one-time goods shed, to form a splendid patio which looks over a sunk garden, only partially filled in from the level of the trackbed.

At the front of the house a less private garden has been imaginatively created out of a vast sweep of land where once were the goods yard and sidings. This is now a large lawn, set with trees and shrubs and roses – a delightful approach for the doctor's patients.

When Tom and Doreen Berriman bought Gilling station, its land and goods shed in 1974, they were not especially keen on a railway house, although they found that no less than three were on the market at the time. They were looking for a pig farm. As it happened, the goods shed and grounds at Gilling had already been modified to accommodate pigs, and so they thought that the house 'would do'.

Nine years later, the Berrimans have come to appreciate the unusual attraction of their property. Working in the garden, they are by now well-accustomed to people leaning over the fence to gaze nostagically at – not one, but two platforms, with a sunk lawn between, unmistakeably a place where trains once ran. Along the platform beside the house is an equally unmistakeable station canopy, with the typical wooden barge boarding, still shading what was once the ladies' room. The latter is now their spare bedroom, but no longer entered from the platform.

Even more conducive to nostalgia, and on the outer wall of what used to be the waiting-room which is now their sitting-room, is the station clock set into the wall and framed by a stone surround. Inside the house is the other clock-face and its works, housed in a long, white-painted case, like a grandfather clock. It still keeps good 'railway time.'

From the junction beyond Gilling, the Pickering and Seamer line took a sweeping curve east and north, then west again, towards Helmsley, with an intermediate station at Nunnington.

Below left:
Slingsby station, on the North Eastern Railway's Gilling–Malton line, in the early years of the century. *Dorothy Cowlin*

Below:
A scene at Pilmoor, on the York–Darlington main line, with 'V2' 2-6-2 No 60976 swinging on to the Malton branch with the 8.5am Glasgow Queen St–Scarborough on 21 July 1962. By then, only through summer Saturday passenger services worked over the Malton line, in addition to local freight trains. A derailment on the main line resulted in the junction being removed as plain track was used for renewal, and for the summer of 1963 (and thereafter), the trains to/from Scarborough ran via York.
J.M. Rayner

In 1964, the railwayman in charge of Nunnington was a Mr Atkinson, who had been there since 1927. He hadn't chosen to buy the house where he had lived with his family all those years. It was more than a mile from the village. When they were young, the family thought nothing of cycling into Nunnington to the shops. On Fridays, Mrs Atkinson had been privileged to travel free by rail into Helmsley for the market. But by 1964 the Atkinsons were elderly. With no railway to Helmsley and not possessing a car, with only one shop in Nunnington village things wouldn't be so easy. They retired elsewhere.

After some years as a café, Nunnington station was transformed into a hotel, and called Ryedale Lodge. A ground-floor room was added in front of what had been the booking hall. Extra bedrooms were added to the original three; these bedrooms later each being provided with individual bathrooms.

John and Janet Laird bought Ryedale Lodge in 1980, and were at first amazed at the interest shown by guests in the history of the hotel. For railway enthusiasts, the small weigh-house to the west of the site is a delightful feature of the scene. The first thing many guests do after arrival is to go out at the back and gaze up and down the old platform, with the grassy track between now studded with cowslips in the spring, as if in hope of a ghost train.

All five of the converted stations I have described are extremely attractive. But the one at Helmsley is probably the most impressive – and also the closest to its original state.

One of the objectors to the Gilling-Pickering line had been a local landowner, the Earl of Feversham. Perhaps he had ensured that the station should be placed well away from his estate, and on the edge of the little town. Once accepted, the station was recognised as a valuable facility, and the special dignity of Helmsley station may be connected with the fact that the Earl's distinguished guests detrained there for Duncombe Park. The station had no less than *five* waiting-rooms: ladies', first and third-class, gentlemen's, first and third-class, and a general waiting-room cum booking office.

The house is still obviously a Victorian railway building. Well-proportioned dormer windows jut out from a slate-covered roof adorned with ornamental edging. There are five massive chimney stacks. From the eaves, there hangs the typical Victorian wooden station canopy. Adorning the roof-ridges is an equally Victorian 'coxcomb' of iron. Yet as a whole the effect is neither fussy nor utilitarian. In the forecourt, where passengers once entered the booking hall, there is a Victorian-style lamp-post, with modern lantern.

When Helmsley station and its master became redundant, the dignified house stood empty for a while, except for two elderly ladies who occupied part of it as a flat, rented from British Railways.

The early promoters had built well. When George Buffoni bought the station for his printing business in the early 1970s, it was still in good condition and the interior was perfectly dry.

Printing is carried out in a new, purpose-built shed away from the house. The signalbox has become a store-room for materials. But the five waiting-rooms, knocked into one, make a splendidly spacious office, well-lit by the Victorian sash windows along both sides. They now frame a view, on the east and onetime platform side, of a tranquil, Ryedale scene of sheep and pasture and small copses, where once coiled swathes of locomotive smoke.

Lancashire and Yorkshire today

D. Ratcliffe

IN THE 1880s, the Lancashire & Yorkshire Railway embarked upon an impressive catalogue of new works: major stations were rebuilt, more powerful locomotives developed and a new line constructed. This comprised two sections: the 13 miles from Windsor Bridge Junction, Salford, to Crow Nest Junction on the outskirts of Wigan, and the four-mile 'Pemberton Loop'. The line was built so that the L&YR's crack Manchester-Liverpool expresses could by-pass Bolton and Wigan and so compete with the London & North Western's route between the two cities over Chat Moss. Timings of 45 mins were introduced, and by 1900 receipts were up by over 50%. Much has changed since those heady days of railway optimism. Rationalisation of services in the 1960s dealt the L&Y route a heavy blow, and through trains are now only a memory. Just the local service to Kirkby survives, and even this demands that passengers change at Wigan.

Determined to see just what was left of this once-famous line, I arrived at Manchester Victoria one morning in January 1983 to catch the 08.08 to Southport, with the intention of travelling as far as Wigan. Victoria station, its exterior cleaned in 1979, is an impressive sight to the traveller who toils up

Hunt's Bank. Its massive frontage, built in 1909, towers over the original building of the Manchester & Leeds Railway, designed by Robert Stephenson in 1844. Inside, the passenger with time to spare can study the tiled wall-map which shows the extent of the Lancashire & Yorkshire's system. Rather ironically, the LNWR's Trans-Pennine route, now Victoria's premier service, is not included. After enjoying a cup of coffee in the charming Edwardian refreshment room, I made my way to the east end of Platform 11 to await the train.

At 08.02, a Birmingham RCW built Class 110 diesel multiple-unit arrived to my surprise from Cheetham Hill sidings. These powerful sets are normally seen only on the through services from Leeds to Southport introduced in 1980; local services are usually the province of Newton Heath-based diesel sets. The first stage of the journey is full of sad reminders of a glorious past. On the left, there are the still-surviving platforms of Exchange station, closed in 1969; on the right is the derelict Irwell Bridge signalbox. Salford station remains open, though served at peak times only, but freight facilities in the area have almost completely disappeared.

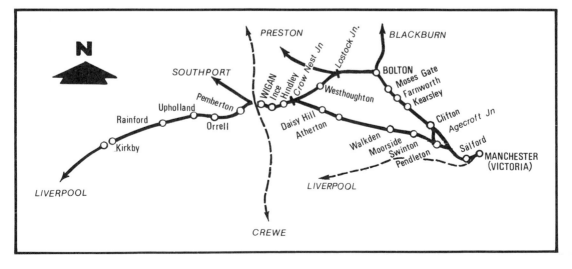

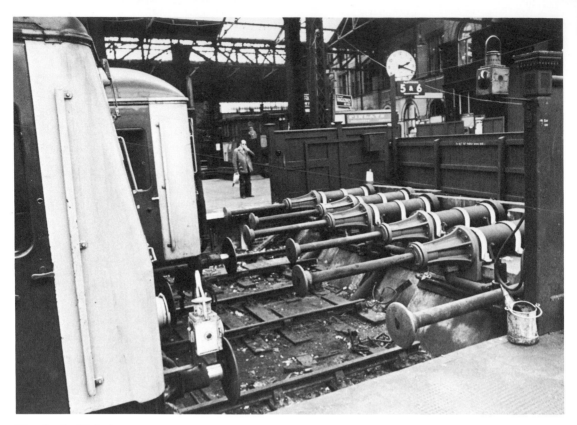

Manchester Victoria:

Above:
Hydraulic buffers and diesel units. February 1978.
Rodney Wildsmith

Right:
The Lancashire & Yorkshire system map, and World War 1 memorial. *N.D. Griffiths*

The Low Level goods depot, reached by a 1 in 27 incline from Oldfield Rd, closed in 1967 when traffic was concentrated at Ardwick and Ashburys in South Manchester. The decline of wagonload traffic has seen Windsor Bridge sidings, once the scene of 24-hr activity with express freights departing to Leeds, Liverpool and Carlisle, reduced to service by a single trip working from Dewsnap Yard, and that runs only as required. Although Hope St Wagon Works closed in 1981 when such repairs were transferred to Horwich, it was gratifying to see a rake of privately-owned wagons in the adjacent roadstone terminal. Aggregates have become an important traffic for rail in the north-west, and block-trains of crushed limestone run daily from the Peakstone Co quarry at Doveholes, near Buxton, to Hope St.

At Windsor Bridge Junction, the diesel unit swung westwards on to the 1888-built line, and ground to a halt at Pendleton Broad St. Although only one island platform remains in use – the fast lines having been removed in 1965 – this station is well-served, not only by Wigan trains but also by those from Blackburn which run over the loop from Agecroft Junction rather than taking the direct line to Windsor Bridge. The climb to Moorside, which begins immediately on leaving Pendleton, is first at 1 in 92 past Brindle scrapyard, then steepens to 1 in 84 beyond Brindle Heath Junction. This section presented no difficulty to the Rolls-Royce engined Class 110 set as it swept past the overgrown platform at Irlam o'th' Heights, closed in March 1956. On the right, there is a fine view of the Irwell Valley, dominated by Agecroft Colliery at which industrial steam locomotives survived until September 1981. Then the line enters the 200yd Pendlebury Tunnel – the only one on the way to Wigan.

Emerging from the western portal, the floodlights of Swinton Rugby League ground, venue for many Challenge Cup semi-finals, are visible in the distance. Swinton retains its typical L&Y station building built on the roadbridge overhead, but the signalbox was taken out of use in 1981 and its upper quadrant signals permanently pulled 'off', so further reducing the capacity of the line. In less than a mile, the train reaches Moorside, the only station on the line to have lost its original buildings; bus-type shelters now provide cover for its few passengers. The train next passed beneath the M62 motorway before running on to an embankment high above Walkden. Rather surprisingly, the first railway into this important mining area was not built until 1875 when the LNWR opened its branch from Manchester Exchange to Bolton Great Moor St. Walkden Low Level was an unusual station, being approached by no less than four sloping footways; it closed in 1954 and now only the L&YR's Walkden High Level remains. This has always been an important stop for local trains and continues to be patronised by many commuters to Manchester and Wigan alike.

The next 3½ miles to Allerton were always

Above:
The Greater Manchester Council's company train conveying the city's refuse from Newton Heath to Appley Bridge passes Agecroft Colliery behind Class 47 No 47.074 on 20 May 1983. *Richard G. Fox*

Below:
Pendleton station in 1982, with a Manchester–Blackburn service departing. *John G. Glover*

regarded as something of a 'race-track' in steam days, and speeds of 75mph were commonplace when the Liverpool expresses were handled by Aspinall's celebrated Atlantics; nowadays the fastest-timed dmus reach no more than 45mph. Faster timings would be possible with improved rolling stock but are unlikely to materialise. The dip in the line at Allerton can cause problems with the ageing dmus, for all services stop at this station, including the few remaining Southport 'fasts'. Outside the peak-hours, the service is two-hourly only, for many Southport trains once more run the 'long way round' to serve Bolton. Allerton goods yard signalbox, the only one between Windsor Bridge and Crow Nest, remains open, but the goods yard, as with all the others on the line, has been closed. Even the tiny amount of freight remaining nowadays takes the Bolton line to Wigan.

As the train nears Crow Nest Junction, it passes the site of Dobbs Brow Junction, where a section of the former trackbed to Horwich Fork Junction is still evident. Like so many in the area, this line closed in 1965 and had been used by Blackpool expresses to by-pass Bolton, although severely graded. The original signalbox at Crow Nest, built in the fork of the lines to Bolton and Manchester, has been replaced by a smaller, modern structure 100 yards further west; semaphore signals so far on

the route give way to colour-lights between here and Wigan. Past Hindley and Ince, any chance of speed is curtailed by numerous mining subsidence slacks, and the scenery is increasingly dominated by reminders of Wigan's industrial past. From the 16th century until World War 1, the area was a major source of coal, but today most pits are worked out and the network of lines in the area which served them has disappeared, Also gone is Hindley No 3 signalbox and the Pemberton Loop, so all trains must use the Ince line into Wigan Wallgate. Wallgate is a neat, attractive station, having a single, wide island platform into which is set a bay, now used by the diesel unit for the Kirkby 'shuttle'. As I arrived, a Class 47 locomotive passed through on the Speedlink freight from Warrington to Westhoughton – an unexpected modern service to find on what is essentially an outdated line. My thoughts were interrupted as a Class 86 roared past on the nearby West Coast main line. I wonder if the Lancashire and Yorkshire will ever see 25kV ac overhead wires?

Wigan Wallgate station:

Right:
A Class 105 diesel unit stands in the bay, waiting to depart as the 17.44 to Kirkby on 26 June 1978.

Below:
Another Class 105 set pulls away from the station on the same date, forming the 17.07 Kirkby–Bolton. *Both: David A. Flitcroft*

A Victorian trio

Alex Rankin

AMONG THE exhibits awaiting restoration at the Steamport, Southport railway museum is Mersey Railway No 5 *Cecil Raikes*. This 0-6-4T is the last of its type, as well as the only surviving locomotive from that Company in Britain, although a sister engine is preserved in New South Wales, Australia.

Who was Cecil Raikes, I wondered? The answer came from a surprising source, but in finding it, other names appeared which shed new light on certain well-known railway personalities from the end of the last century.

The real cause of the search was the passage through my hands at work of a document which referred to 'Henry Cecil Raikes, Her Majesty's Postmaster-General.' Was this our man?

In *Railway World's* March and April 1976 issues, C.P. Atkins outlined the history of the Mersey Railway's tank engines. He referred to Cecil Raikes as Secretary of the Company and an MP. I decided to study various magazines to see what was there. *The Locomotive* was fruitful, but there were two separate references to his position. In the November 1934 issue, on page 343, he was described as Deputy Chairman, while in the August 1931 issue on page 270 Raikes was described as Chairman.

The emphasis on Raikes switched to the *Railway Magazine*, page 633 of the September 1952 issue where H.C. Casserley described Mersey Railway 0-6-4T No 5, still then at work under the auspices of the National Coal Board. After a search, the January 1953 issue on page 68 produced a note by R.S McNaught who was employed by the then General Post Office at Spalding, and who remembered the Mersey Railway locomotives in service. He wrote that Henry Cecil Raikes was MP for Chester. From 1874-77, he was Deputy Speaker

Below:
The former Mersey Railway 0-6-4T No 5 *Cecil Raikes* **was withdrawn for preservation from service with the National Coal Board. It is seen with a train of empties bound for Shipley Colliery, Derbyshire on 10 June 1953.**

for the House of Commons. He was then Postmaster-General from 1877-91, until his death. A stone bearing his name is to be seen on the Angel Street corner of the GPO in St Martins le Grand, London. This was unveiled in 1890 to commemorate the jubilee of the penny inland post. The building still stands and Raikes' portrait is displayed inside, in common with that of all Postmaster-Generals.

Also in 1890, Raikes found himself under attack from Post Office staff. In 1889, discontent had led to the setting-up of the Postmans' Union. In June 1890, there was a huge demonstration in Hyde Park, followed in July by a march on St Martin's-le-Grand by the men from the Eastern District Office. As a result of the second demonstration, 435 men were dismissed. Memorials were received from postmen throughout the country, and so Raikes decided to set up a committee which was headed by Herbert Joyce. The outcome was a rise of 2/-(10p) in the weekly wage for postmen in London, to 34s (£1.70) and rural postmen were given two weeks holiday!

Raikes' other great battle was with Henniker Heaton who fought long and hard for postal reform, but Raikes died seven years or so before Heaton's efforts were rewarded.

At this point, it is as well to detail the postal and telephone businesses as they then existed. As today, postal and telecommunications were separate operations. The Post Office handled post, while the telegraph business had bought out the railway companies' telegraph services some years earlier. The telephone system was operated by various

companies. One of the largest was the National Telephone Company, but the Post Office acted to regulate licences for these companies to operate.

Now, on a previous occasion, I had read the obituary of Alfred Rosling Bennett which appeared in the July 1928 *Locomotive*. Today, Bennett is remembered for *The Chronicles of Boulton's Siding*, reprinted as recently as 1971 by David and Charles. Bennett was a telephone and telegraph engineer by profession. In 1880, he was appointed Engineering Superintendent of the East London District of the United Telephone Co and, in 1881, he patented various pieces of telephone equipment. From this point, there is a direct link with the third individual in this story, but we will complete Bennett's story first.

In 1883, he joined the National Telephone Co as engineer for Scotland and Ireland, later becoming General Manager for Scotland and North West England. In 1890, an exhibition was staged to coincide with the opening of the Forth Bridge. Bennett's own account of the setting-up of the Railway Pavilion was published posthumously in the October 1928 *Locomotive* on pages 320-23.

F.W. Webb of the London & North Western Railway agreed to send a locomotive to the exhibition, and Bennett was asked for a suitable name for the exhibit. Subsequently, Webb himself named the locomotive *Jeannie Deans* – it was to become very famous, working the 2pm 'Corridor' express out of Euston for many years. Stirling of the Great Northern Railway sent No 776 of the 8ft driving wheel Single type, on condition it went through to Edinburgh under its own steam. In the process, it almost lost its chimney at the Meadowbank bridge which carries what is now the A1 road over the railway! Incidentally, North Eastern Railway No 1521 was also sent to the exhibition and the NER demanded (but was refused) permission to run a trial trip over the North British line to Perth!

In 1891, Bennett read a paper at the British Association meeting at Cardiff on the subject of 'An Electrical Parcel Exchange'. The idea behind it was one that largely materialised in 1928 as the Post Office Underground Railway. Bennett wrote to the *Locomotive* magazine and his letter appeared on page 169 of the May 1928 issue, referring to this paper. In the letter, he mentions that Sir William Preece, the Post Office Chief Engineer, was a member of the BA committee when his paper was accepted. Preece's successor, Sir John Garvey, had heard Bennett's delivery of the paper. That Preece had been involved in another engineering paper come to light subsequently.

Bennett subsequently obtained the licence for the Guernsey Telephone Service in 1895, despite opposition from the Post Office and was later involved in telephone services in Glasgow, Tunbridge Wells, Portsmouth, Brighton and Hull, having left the National Telephone Co to promote them, obtain the licences and operate them. However, it was through the National Telephone Company that the third member of the trio forming the subject of this study appears. His name – James Staats Forbes.

Forbes was born in Aberdeen. After an early career on the Great Western Railway, he moved to the Dutch Rhenish Railway which was built to 6ft 4in gauge. It was from here that our most exotic connection appears. In the November 1982 issue of the *Railway Magazine*, George Behrend speculated on the fact that Forbes was named as a director of Mann's Railway Sleeping Carriage Co of 1873, along with Mann & Nagelmackers. Forbes gave Nagelmackers his first contract in 1873 on the Dutch Rhenish Railway and persuaded the Belgian Railways to do the same. In 1876, Nagelmackers bought out Colonel Mann to form the Wagons-Lits Co, but there is no evidence of Forbes being on the board thereafter. There was, however, the Club Train episode on the London, Chatham & Dover Railway in 1889 when a complete Wagons-Lits train was shipped over to Britain and operated on the LC&DR in connection with a special boat on the Dover-Calais crossing. The whole thing was a monumental flop, and the coaches ended their days in Belgium, some lasting until 1925, being distinguishable by their small size.

In 1880, the United Telephone Company was formed with James Staats Forbes as Vice-Chairman. Alfred Rosling Bennett was in charge of underground and overhead lines in what was termed the London Docks area. Interestingly enough, in Baldwin's *History of the Telephone in the UK*, the area external engineers are listed by surnames, only Bennett being described as A.R Bennett! Another name of interest which appears is C.E. Spagnoletti, who worked for the Great Western Railway until 1889 when he became consulting engineer for the City & South London Railway until his retirement in 1892. He was responsible for the telegraph systems of the Metropolitan and District Railways, among other work in the telegraph and telephone industries.

In 1883, the National Telephone Company was formed with James Staats Forbes as Chairman, a position he held until 1900. From 1901, he was President, a position he held until his death in 1904. In February 1884, the Society of Telegraph Engineers and Electricians heard a paper on an experiment in 1883 when Forbes had equipped a train with electric light. A small engine with dynamo was fitted to a locomotive which supplied steam for its operation. The idea was tried out on the District Railway using an LC&DR parcels van borrowed (or lent) for the occasion. No batteries were used.

At that time, battery power was used for lighting on several railways, including the Midland, Great Northern, South Eastern and London & South Western. The fact that the South Eastern used primary batteries perhaps explains why this experiment was undertaken! Among those who commented on the paper at length was Sir William Preece, the Post Office Chief Engineer.

One unanswered question, who read the paper? Was it Bennett? Incidentally, the problem of this

Memorials to the railway interests of Cecil Raikes and Rosling Bennett:

Above:
The Post Office Railway in London was opened in 1928, the year of Rosling Bennett's death. He had outlined the principles of such a system in 1891.
Post Office/Crown Copyright

Above right:
When Raikes was Postmaster-General, the first all-postal West Coast TPO train was introduced, in 1885. This shows the interior of a TPO vehicle, LMS No 30246, in 1947. *BR*

form of lighting was that when the locomotive was uncoupled, the train was left without lighting!

In 1895, James Staats Forbes was one of the leading witnesses at the Tweedmouth enquiry into the telephone service. It appears that the findings of this enquiry may have been one of the reasons why Bennett had quite a battle to get the licence for the Guernsey Telephone Service.

Bennett as General Manager of the National Telephone Co would have been responsible to Forbes as Chairman and, later, President. I suspect that Forbes' death in 1904 was the reason for Bennett's departure to pastures new. Forbes, in turn, would have dealt with Raikes on Parliamentary business.

The three men between them undertook much of the spadework for what is today British Telecom, but they also left other probably better-known memorials among railway enthusiasts.

Forbes' idea for a Club train was resurrected in 1926, becoming the 'Golden Arrow' which lasted until the 1970s, while in 1936, the Night Ferry

started, the only Wagons-Lits sleeping car train to run in Britain, and which disappeared in 1980.

Raikes, too, has a train to serve as a reminder of his works. On 1 July 1885, the first all-postal mail train left Euston at 8.30pm for Aberdeen, thereby inaugurating the famed 'West Coast Postal'. Previously passengers had been carried on the predecessor of this service, but henceforth passengers travelled on a separate train which in 1895 was to race its East Coast rival from London to Aberdeen.

Thus, 1985/86 by rights should see some commemoration of Raikes, the three centenaries between 1 July and 20 January being as follows:
1 July – 'West Coast Postal' as separate Mail Train.
2 January – Mersey Railway No 5 *Cecil Raikes*.
20 January – Mersey Railway opened between Liverpool and Birkenhead.

We are fortunate that No 5 still exists. After all, it was one of the most powerful engines in Britain at the time it was built and fortunately retains its condensing gear. One hopes that it will be restored for its centenary.

I must express my thanks to the following for their assistance: John Benson, for getting me interested initially; British Telecom Scotland, where the first clue was unearthed; the Scottish Postal Board, where a senior member of staff cleared up one or two points about St Martins-le-Grand, and the Telecom Technology Showcase in London where Mr Armstrong unearthed and forwarded some very interesting snippets on Raikes and Forbes. The various magazine references are from my personal collection.

Marylebone steam
Photo feature

The future of Marylebone station, London is currently in some doubt. It looks unlikely to celebrate its centenary in its present form. For three-quarters of a century the station has been a quiet haven, since 1966 no more than a terminus for outer suburban trains running no further than to Banbury, and to High Wycombe and Aylesbury. One of the periods of activity was in the late 1940s, when Marylebone was served by the 'Master Cutler' and 'South Yorkshireman' express trains, and in 1948 locomotives of designs built by all the 'Big Four' companies appeared in the terminus on the famed Locomotive Exchanges of that year. From then, the moments of glory became increasingly fewer . . .

Below:
Construction of the approaches to the capital of the London Extension of the Great Central Railway (it assumed that title on 1 August 1897, previously the Manchester, Sheffield and Lincolnshire Railway) began in 1895. To make way, over 1,000 houses were demolished. Marylebone station has four platforms (950ft long) served by five lines. The buildings were made capable of carrying two more floors, and, on the western side, provision was made for the extension of the station. The inaugural special trains ran into the terminus for the opening ceremony on 9 March 1899. Passenger services began on 15 March that year. A general view of the country end of the station, soon after opening. *LPC/Ian Allan Library*

Above:
Ian Allan Ltd organised an excursion from Marylebone on 12 May 1956 to Sheffield, Manchester, Barnsley and returning to King's Cross, distinguished by its all-Pullman car accommodation. 'A4' 4-6-2 No 60014 *Silver Link*, before departure of the special. *D.V. Abbott*

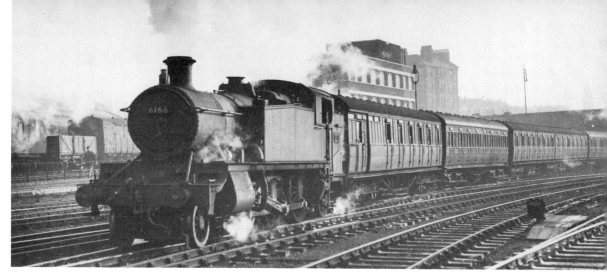

Left:
On 11 June 1948, 'West Country' 4-6-2 No 34006 *Bude* approaches Marylebone with an express from Manchester London Road during the Locomotive Exchanges. Note the dynamometer car behind the borrowed LMS-design tender (fitted with a water scoop). *F.R. Hebron/Rail Archive Stephenson*

Below left:
First making regular appearances out of Marylebone in 1938, when Gresley Pacifics returned to the GC main line after World War 2, 'A3s' were employed. On the down 'Master Cutler', No 60052 *Prince Palatine* sets out for Sheffield during July 1952. Milk tank wagons working from the Shrewsbury area can be seen to the left. *Brian Morrison*

Top:
The suburban services from Paddington to High Wycombe were transferred to run into/out of Marylebone shortly after nationalisation. In time, the Western Region, and then the London Midland Region took over control of the London end of the GC main line from the Eastern Region. For a short time, WR '61xx' 2-6-2Ts worked to Marylebone, such as No 6166 with the 12.20pm to Princes Risborough on 14 December 1949. *C.C.B. Herbert*

Above right:
From the start of 1960, daytime main line trains to/from Marylebone were limited to three semi-fast services each way from/to Nottingham Victoria. In 1963, the Sunday semi-fasts were withdrawn, and the end for the other trains – and for most of the GC's London Extension – came on 3 September 1966. On this last day, LMS '5' 4-6-0 No 45292 turns at Marylebone before working the last down semi-fast. The turntable remains in situ today. *K.P. Lawrence*

Right:
There have been suggestions that steam should once more grace Marylebone, on main line specials to Stratford-upon-Avon. This seems unlikely, and the nearest to a steam revival came in August 1974 when the Great Western Society's '43xx' 2-6-0 No 5322 was hauled to the terminus for the filming of the motion picture *One of our Dinosaurs is Missing*.
Great Western Society

The Settle & Carlisle by night

G. L. Pallister

NIGHT fell early. It had been far from bright all day, and by 3.30pm the darkness was fast closing-in and a light drizzle set in. We reached the station at about 4.45pm and walked on to the up platform. At intervals along its length, gas-lamps flared, casting small pools of brightness around them, interspersed by comparative darkness. On our left were the station buildings, two blocks extending out at right-angles to the platform with a long block between them containing the booking hall. On the outside of these buildings were several notices, all hand-written, one to the effect that the station staff would be glad to see anyone on matters of business. On the maroon-painted door of the booking hall, identified by the words Booking Hall inscribed in white letters upon it, was a list of train departures, also hand-written. We pushed open the door and stepped inside a rectangular room with benches against the longer sides. On the north wall a large fireplace contained the dying embers of a fire; by it, sat an old man reading a newspaper and muttering to himself.

Above the fireplace hung several certificates awarded to Settle in the station gardens competition. At the south end of the room was the window of the booking office. For a short time, we sat in the pleasant warmth, then went out on to the platform and walked to the south end, where there was a large board proclaiming Settle's vital statistics. including its population size, height above sea level and distances to London and Carlisle.

We walked back along the platform, past the neatly-kept buldings and down the platform-end, from which a number of wooden boards crossed the track. Looking northwards towards Horton, a red signal-lamp could be seen just beyond the station. Then, across the lines, and we walked on to the down platform, passing at the end the weird shape of a water crane. On this platform was a single small

Below:
Settle station, looking north on 6 July 1964.
G.L. Pallister

Above:
On 1 August 1964, the train featuring in the article, the 3.40pm Bradford Forster Square–Carlisle stopping train approaches Batty Moss Viaduct, Ribblehead. *A.W. Martin*

building, the waiting room, and as we approached it the porter called cheerily across from the other side, 'There's a lamp inside – just pull the lever.' Opening the door, hanging from the ceiling inside was a large gas-lamp, its pilot light burning dimly. My father, familiar with such contraptions from his youth, pulled a thin metal rod which hung down from the lamp. At first nothing happened, then he blew vigorously, the gas ignited and the light flared up. The building was rectangular with a bench along one side and a stone floor. It was a cold as a vault and our breath blew out in great clouds in the damp air. A little after 5 pm, we went out on to the platform again.

The sky was completely dark and a gusty wind blew from the south west, bringing with it a fine, wetting drizzle. To the south, a faint blur of lights indicated the presence of a signalbox. Looking around the station on this dark winter's night it was indeed hard to imagine that the scene had changed since the opening of the line in the 1870s.

A bell rang loudly on the up platform. The porter and a couple of passengers were crossing the line and, to the north, the signal-lamp was green. Very faintly, far away on the night air, there was a low rumbling. I peered down the line but could see nothing. The rumbling grew louder, and then I discerned a faint glow moving towards us. The noice increased and a black shape rumbled out of the darkness. The station lamps revealed the rugged profile of a 'Jubilee' 4-6-0 No 45588 *Kashmir* which had given me a run from Carlisle to Dumfries the previous February. The train halted. The porter opened a door at the end of the first coach, a relatively new BR standard corridor vehicle. The

train was made up of a parcel van at the front, four passenger coaches, a parcels van and two four-wheeled vans at the rear.

At 5.19 pm, there was a cry from the platform, then a loud hiss from the engine which puffed slowly out. The station lamps vanished, then for a fleeting instant the lights of Settle were below us, illuminating grey roofs wet with drizzle. Soon, we were out into a winter night climbing into the Pennines. For a few minutes I sat in the brightly-lit compartment listening to the exhaust-beats of the engine as they grew faster and fainter. But on a journey like this there was only one place to be – out in the corridor!

I lowered a window and leaned out. The cold, damp air blew in my face and the drizzle wetted my glasses. Ahead, a bright orange glare shone from the 'Jubilee's' cab, lighting up the exhaust which billowed from the chimney and, at the same time, revealing the great, rough-hewn walls of the rock cutting through which we were passing. I crossed to the other side of the vestibule. On leaning out, I was enveloped in steam, and at first could see little. Then the cutting walls were gone and, instead, the light from the carriages indicated a bare stretch of grass alongside the track. Beyond, the moorland was hidden by the darkness. The brakes came on and a glow of oil-lamps announced the entry to

Horton station. The engine hissed gently for a few seconds, then loudly puffed away. I leaned out once more. Steam swirled past and I smelt the sulphurous fumes of coal-smoke. Against the pitch black of the sky, a steady procession of sparks floated past, falling slowly and gracefully earthwards. The train now swung westwards, dim oil-lamps once more appeared, the brakes were applied and we pulled violently to a halt at Ribblehead station. Somewhere down the train a door slammed. Then a voice from the darkness cried, 'Right-away, Jack.' A short, deep whistle came from the engine and the train pulled out. Almost at once, the 'Jubilee' slipped on the wet rails and the orderly puffing degenerated into a jumble. But the driving wheels gripped and the three-cylinder beat resumed. We turned towards Batty Moss Viaduct and I looked back at the line of lighted carriages. Just before the Viaduct, the 'Jubilee' lost adhesion completely, there was a loud bellowing and a shower of yellow sparks shot from below the driving wheels. Having recovered, seconds later the 'Jubilee' was blasting over the viaduct to the accompaniment of a display of sparks shooting out of the chimney, to fall slowly into the valley below. A blur of lights soon appeared and through the swirling steam I glimpsed Blea Moor signalbox with its signalman at the lever-frame. Crossing to the other side, a ball of fire seemed to leap up at me and I darted back into the corridor. Looking back, I saw a brazier of flaming coals beneath the water-crane in Blea Moor loop!

Now we were on the last stretch of the long 1 in 100 climb from Settle. The cutting walls rose higher and higher, they overwhelmed us and the train entered the clammy depths of Blea Moor Tunnel. I gingerly lowered a window on the right-hand side, at once smelling the damp, suffocating air in the tunnel while the glow from the firedoor lit up the great brick arch of the tunnel roof, covered by a black slime which reflected a reddish tinge. Here, in this strange world deep below the wild Pennine moors, the fascination of railways was at its strongest – something almost infernal which rooted my attention.

Before long, speed increased, indicating that we had reached the summit of the climb from Settle

Top left:
The 3.40pm from Bradford Forster Square, again, this time entering Dent station on 11 July 1964 behind 'Rebuilt Jubilee' 4-6-0 No 45736 *Phoenix.*
Paul Riley

Bottom left:
No longer used by trains appearing in the public timetable, Horton in Ribblesdale was still patronised by the summer Dalesrail trains when photographed in 1983. A Class 40 approaches with an up parcels train. *K. Groundwater*

Junction and now we were outside on a desolate hillside that descended steeply from the mist-clad moors to the dark, deep valley below. The train rattled briskly along the wild hillside, then passed Dent signalbox, and as the brakes ground on and the oil-lamps swung into view, I heard a strange, almost plaintive, cry: 'Dent! Dent!' It was incredible that anyone should alight at such a God-forsaken place. Almost at once we were away and soon in the confines of Rise Hill Tunnel. I walked down the train. There was no one else in the leading coach and only three passengers in the next, two of them railwaymen.

The train came to a halt in Garsdale, the last of the mountain stations, and after a short stop was back into the night. A sudden noise and the blur of lights on the other track were revealed as the 4.37 pm stopping train from Carlisle. And so as we accelerated away from Ais Gill below the mist-clad summit of Wild Boar Fell, I left the corridor and retired to the brightness and warmth of the compartment. The train rolled on steadily through the succession of tunnels and, a little after 6.15 pm, we pulled up at Kirkby Stephen West station. *Kashmir* put on speed from the restart and made a brisk run to Appleby.

From Appleby West station, the 'Jubilee' was soon taking the almost empty train at a good speed through the Eden Valley. The rain had now ceased, but the night was pitch-black and nothing could be seen through the windows, apart from the occasional glow from a farmhouse. The engine blew-off on the falling gradients and occasional sparks drifted past. The little stations — Long Marton, New Biggin, Culgaith, Langwathby, Little Salkeld, Lazonby and Armathwaite — came in succession, the train stopping briskly, and briefly at each of them. As we journeyed on, I savoured the many familiar sounds: the short, deep hoot from the whistle before departure from each station, the sound of steam blowing-off between Little Salkeld and Lazonby, the scrape of the fireman's shovel at Langwathby, the roaring syncopation in the tunnels, and the steady rhythm of wheelsets over rail-joints.

There was a short whistle and *Kashmir* puffed away from Armathwaite. For once, the exhaust-beats did not die away, but stayed loud and hard and an orange glare shone brightly from the cab as we tackled the last stretch of the Settle and Carlisle. After some fast running, scattered lights appeared, then sidings and points, and signalboxes and buildings. Yards appeared and we clattered over the junction with the Newcastle line at Petteril Bridge Junction. Speed fell and we came slowly up the bank into Carlisle's Platform 5 to halt on time at 7.29 pm. We alighted, paid our respects to the 'Jubilee', and so ended an atmospheric journey over the always-memorable metals of the Settle and Carlisle line.

Railway postcards
A. M. Goodbody

THE VERY early history of postcards showing railway subjects or having railway connections is shrouded in some obscurity. Court cards (4½in x 3½in) issued by the Caledonian Railway Company's Central Hotel in Glasgow date from the 1890s, while a court card issued by the then recently opened Snowdon Mountain Tramroad is known to have appeared in the summer of 1897. The first well-known card depicting a railway subject was a triple vignette court card produced by the Locomotive Publishing Company and showing scenes from the Great Northern Railway. This card is believed to have been issued in 1897 or 1898.

The advent in Britain of the picture postcard in its familiar form dates from 1 November 1899. This date was when the Post Office after a long campaign by Messrs Raphael Tuck & Sons at last allowed the

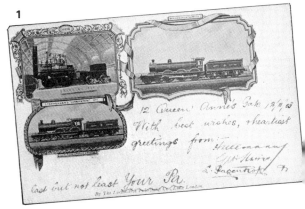

Figs 1/2. *Collection of A.M. Goodbody*

standard sized postcard (5½ in x 3½ in) to be sent through the post.

Armed with advance knowledge of the Post Office's change of policy, Tuck was the first to produce standard sized cards, but the Locomotive Publishing Company was probably the first in the field with railway subjects. Two more vignette cards, similar to the original court card but of standard size, appeared in 1900. One of these commemorated the Diamond Jubilee of the London and North Western Railway while the other showed scenes from the North Eastern Railway (Fig 1).

Tuck was best-known for the Company's coloured 'Oilettes' which made their appearance in December 1904, but the firm also produced over 100 'Official' cards for the London & North Western Railway. Subjects included locomotives, rolling stock, bridges, steamships and places of interest served by the Railway. There were about 14 sets of six cards and a number of odd cards; they were sold for 2d per set of six. One of these cards, No 15-0084 (Silvester) of Set 10A (Locomotives – Additional Set), shows the Engineer's inspection coach *Locomotion* (Fig 2).

Before the end of 1904, Tuck had been ousted by McCorquodale as printer of the LNWR's official cards, and the latter went on to produce several hundred different designs up to the outbreak of World War 2, with total sales exceeding 11 million. These cards depicted almost every aspect of railway working. One of the rarest is a vertical format card showing the typewriting room on the Birmingham-London Broad St trains.

Although the LNWR was by far the most prolific publishers of official railway postcards, it was not the only railway company to do so. Experiments with internal combustion were publicised on an official London, Brighton & South Coast Railway card printed by Waterlow & Sons Ltd. (Fig 3). It shows the Company's petrol rail motor car No 4 which ran on the Kemp Town branch in Brighton.

In spite of experiments with electric traction and internal combustion engines during the early years of the century, steam was to reign supreme on railways for a considerable number of years, and it is worth turning our attention to some overseas locomotives shown on postcards. Some of the most attractive and accurate cards of steam locomotives were produced by the works who built them. A very fine example is the card (Fig 4) produced in 1924 by the Prague-based Českomoravská-Kolben Works. It shows the 1,000th locomotive built there, one of 10 2-8-0 locomotives of Class 445.1, later reclassified 455.1. It was printed by Stenc of Prague. In 1912, the Belgian firm of Les Ateliers Métallurgiques; Nivelles, Tubize & La Sambre (later La Brugeoise & Nivelles) was building locomotives for China at its Tubize works. One of

3
Petrol Rail Motor, L.B. & S.C.R.

4

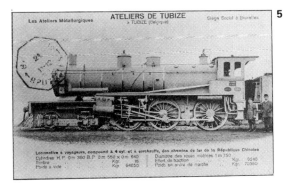
5

6

Figs 3–6. *Collection of A.M. Goodbody*

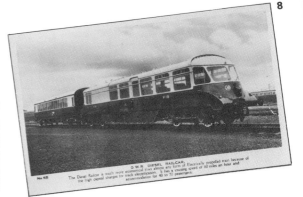

Figs 7–10. *Collection of A.M. Goodbody*

these is shown on the Company's official postcard, complete with technical details on the picture side (Fig 5). The message dated 21 June 1912 and addressed to Mr A.R. Bell, Hotel du Colonies, Brussels advises: 'Our works are closed tomorrow on account of a local fête. Would be pleased to see you on Tuesday.'

Although not a works card, but produced to the same high standard, the card (Fig 6) of a Hungarian State Railway Class 328 locomotive is worthy of mention at this stage. It was published by Kladja a Gözmozdony Vasutés Erögépszaklap, Budapest in 1919 (card No 8259). This class of locomotive has an interesting history. Although designed in Hungary, the first 100 were ordered from Henschel in Germany. Of these, 83 were delivered, but the remaining 17 were seized by the French as war reparations. The French discovered that these engines exceeded their loading gauge and passed them on to Czechoslovakia; some of them eventually reached Hungary in 1939. The Hungarian State Railway works in Budapest built a further 58 between 1919-22, and it is one of these that appears on the card.

The golden age of postcards largely coincided with the golden age of steam. Not surprisingly,

there are far more cards available showing steam locomotives than any other form of motive power. Early cards depicting diesel locomotives are particularly hard to find which is why (Fig 7) showing a six-axle diesel railcar of the Saxon State Railways must be considered a gem. It was published by Johannes Leonhardt of Dresden (card No 2185). The card has no postmark to indicate its date, but presumably was published about 1915, the year given for the construction of the railcar. Technical data is given on the address side of the card and a translation reveals that the diesel engine was built by Sulzer of Winterthur and electrical equipment by Brown, Broweri (sic). This must indeed be Brown, Boveri, the incorrect word sounding remarkably like the German word for brewery! To continue with the technical information, there were 80 seats and room for 10 standing passengers, the overall length was 20135 mm, and the weight empty 64,000 kg.

The firm of Wildt and Kray was not renowned for accurate representations of steam locomotives on its coloured cards; however, the 'real photograph' of the Great Western Railway diesel railcar of the 1930s leaves little to be desired (Fig 8). The next card, showing 'German State Railways Express Railcar, Built Hamburg 1935' (Fig 9) appears to contain an inaccuracy. Hamburg, although an important industrial centre, was not the home of locomotive factories. The original 'Flying

CAMINOS DE HIERRO DEL NORTE DE ESPAÑA

Automotor eléctrico con su remolque

CAMINOS DE HIERRO DEL NORTE DE ESPAÑA

Trenes con tracción eléctrica en la sección Barcelona-Manresa

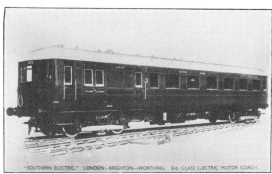

"SOUTHERN ELECTRIC." LONDON—BRIGHTON—WORTHING. 3rd. CLASS ELECTRIC MOTOR COACH.

Figs 11–14. *Collection of A.M. Goodbody*

Hamburger', of which this is a development, was introduced in 1931. Built by WUMAG (Waggon und Maschinenbau AG, Görlitz), it was a two-car articulated unit known as Class VT.04. The card was published by J. Bettenhausen of Dresden.

Electric traction was developed in several European countries including Switzerland, the railway network of which has been almost totally electrified for some years. A card published by Julien Brothers of Geneva (Fig 10) shows electric cars at Champéry, the southern terminus of the 750V dc Aigle-Ollon-Monthey-Champéry Railway. An undated Spanish card published by Huecograbado Mumbrú of Barcelona (Fig 11) is inscribed 'Northern Railway of Spain. Electric Railcar and Trailer.' These multiple-unit sets date from 1929 and worked the 1,500V ac Madrid-Avila-Segovia service.

From the same Spanish publisher comes a card (Fig 12) showing electric locomotives. On the left is a Class 7001, of which 12 were delivered in 1928 by Oerlikon with mechanical parts by Euskalduna. They were C-C wheel arrangement and designed to work at 1,500 V dc. In the same year, 25 of the 1C-C1 Class 7101 (right) were supplied by the same manufacturers. The UK did not go in for electric locomotives to any great extent before World War 2, but there were plenty of electric multiple-units, and the motor coach from one of these is shown on a real photograph card by an unknown publisher (Fig 13).

15

16

17

View of the Northern Entrance to the Station and
Memorial Arch dedicated to the employees of the
London & South Western Railway Company who gave their
lives for King and Country in the Great War, 1914-1918.
Unveiled by Queen Mary, 21st March, 1922.

Figs 15–18. *Collection of A.M. Goodbody*

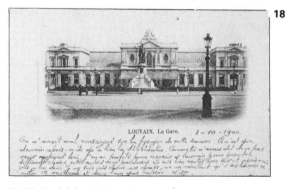

18

Items of rolling stock appear comparatively infrequently in their own right on picture postcards. The main exception is probably the London & North Western Railway, that undertaking producing cards showing a range of passenger coaches, as well as the interior and exterior of travelling post office vans. The Locomotive Publishing Company produced a beautiful coloured card showing a North Eastern Railway snowplough. Shown here is an iron ore bogie hopper wagon built for the Bengal Nagpur Railway in India (Fig 14). The card was published by the builder of the wagon, Cammell Laird of Nottingham.

One of the more interesting items of rolling stock to have been shown on a card was the coach in which the Armistice was signed on 11 November 1918 (Fig 15). The card was published by the Friends of the Army Museum and produced by J. Hauser of Paris. The vehicle was a teak-bodied Wagon Lits dining car No 2419, built 1913/14, and it was apparently destroyed in Germany in 1945.

At one time, cards showing railway stations were commonplace in this country and abroad. Even so, there are some curious gaps. Who, for example, has seen the handsome facade of Chester station on a postcard? The first card (Fig 16) was published by

W.H. Smith in 1922 and shows the main entrance to the then newly rebuilt Waterloo Station. Apart from its obvious use, the entrance serves also as a war memorial and a monument to national pride. The names of countries which figured prominently in the Great War and in earlier campaigns are written round the arch – France, Belgium, Italy, Egypt etc. The symbolic figure above and each side of the arch serve to commemorate the recent victory and the victory at Waterloo in 1815.

In Germany, a rather different war memorial survives to remind us of the ravages of World War 2. The Anhalter Bahnhof in Berlin, shown on the next card (Fig 17), was rebuilt in the 1870s to the design of the architect Franz Schwechten. At one time, it was the terminus not only for Anhalt but also for Frankfurt (Main), Magdeburg and other places to

19

20

21

mysterious LL? The answer was discovered in 1974 by Valerie Monahan, a collector and student of postcards. The initial stood for Louis Levy, who in the case of the card shown here was both photographer and publisher.

Photographic interiors of railway stations are much sought after as they are often the only record of stations in their former state. This interwar view of Leipzig station (Fig 20) is a case in point. Although the facade is extant, the main concourse and train shed had to be rebuilt after World War 2. The legend on the back proclaims simply that the card was distributed by the Leipzig Station Bookshop Co, of which one branch is shown in the photograph. The card was posted from Leipzig to London in 1927.

In contrast to the bustling interior of Leipzig Hauptbahnhof is the little wayside French station at La Valbonne (Fig 21). Small though it was, it was a stopping point for the Lyon à Ambérieux courrier convoyeur, as indicated by the wavy-line cancellation. This term is hard to translate as we have no equivalent in this country. It is a kind of second-class railway travelling post office which runs only when required to handle the volume of mail. The publisher was the local firm of Romand.

Clearly, there is much more about railway postcards than can be included in a short feature; indeed, a volume has been written about the official LNWR cards alone. Then, there are entire categories not touched on here. Bridges, tunnels and signalling have not been mentioned, neither has the vast array of comic cards with a railway flavour. I can only hope that readers will be prompted to discover railway postcards for themselves and perhaps join the ranks of the collectors.

Bibliography

Byatt, A. *Picture Postcards and their Publishers*, Golden Age Postcard Books, Malvern, 1978.

Duval, W. and Monahan, V. *Collecting Postcards in Colour, 1894-1914*, Blandford Press, Poole, 1978.

Mead, R., Venman J., and Whitney J.T. *Picton's Priced Postcard Catalogue and Handbook*, Picton Print, Chippenham.

(NB: This catalogue is published annually, but the 1982 edition is particularly useful as it contains a railway postcard supplement).

Silvester R. *Official Railway Postcards of the British Isles, Part 1, London & North Western Railway, Picton Print. Part 2, Great Western Railway.*

(Further volumes are expected to be published in due course.)

the south and west of Berlin. Today, bereft of function – its tracks were interrupted by the border with East Germany – and lacking train shed and platforms, only the facade remains to remind us of its great past and of the war which was to cause its demise. The card gives no clue as to its publisher.

The card of Louvain station in Belgium (Fig 18) has the added distinction (for the philatelist at least) that it was posted at the station post office on 10 October 1900. Again, the publisher has preferred to remain anonymous. Not so the publisher of the card (Fig 19) of Oran station on the PLM in Algeria. It was Levy Fils & Cie of Paris, and thereby hangs a tale. Cards bearing the initials LL, as seen on the picture side of this card, are frequently encountered. Cards showing scenes from several countries bear these initials, but who was the

Lines to the Tower
Martin Bairstow

A PORT at the mouth of the Wyre destined to rival Liverpool was the idea of Sir Peter Hesketh Fleetwood, MP of Rossall Hall. A company under his chairmanship was formed in 1835 to build a railway from Preston to what became Fleetwood, where it was planned to develop the harbour. The single track Preston & Wyre Railway opened on 15 July 1840. It was worked by the North Union Railway (Bolton/Wigan – Preston) and reached Fleetwood by a two-mile timber trestle viaduct across the Wyre. Connecting steamers operated to Ardrossan, as yet there was no direct railway to Scotland, as well as to Belfast and to Douglas, Isle of Man.

Branch railways to Lytham and to Blackpool were authorised in 1844 to leave the Preston & Wyre main line respectively at Kirkham and Poulton. Both lines opened during 1846 and so began the rapid development of the Fylde coast as a holiday area. Following the joint takeover of the North Union Railway by the Lancashire & Yorkshire and London & North Western Railways in 1846, the Preston & Wyre became vested in those two companies in the ratio of two-thirds and one-third.

Work began in 1846 on doubling the Preston to Fleetwood line and this involved a new route on dry land by-passing the timber viaduct over the Wyre. Progress with the development of Fleetwood Docks was slow but facilities were provided by the L&YR from 1877.

The Blackpool & Lytham Railway, opened in 1863, was initially without connection to any other railway. Its Blackpool terminus was on the Central Promenade adjacent to the future location of the Tower and the Lytham terminus was a short way from the Preston & Wyre station. In 1872, the line was absorbed into the Preston & Wyre, and arrangements were made to link up the two systems in Lytham and for a better junction at Kirkham which shortened the route to Preston. The new arrangements came into use in 1874 and the entire route was double track by 1876. The Blackpool station was at first called Hounds Hill, and renamed Central in 1878. The older Preston & Wyre station became Blackpool Talbot Road to distinguish it from its new rival.

The increasing level of traffic, particularly at

Below:
Blackpool Central station in 1896, the occasion of Bass & Co's mammoth employees excursion from Burton-on-Trent. Nine trains are waiting to load for the return trip. The age of the photograph has meant that the Tower has faded from view! The engines are seemingly all Lancashire & Yorkshire Railway 4-4-0s, and the rolling stock naturally provided by the Midland Railway. *LPC/Ian Allan Library*

holiday peaks, brought about improvements in operating capacity. Quadruple track was completed between Preston and Kirkham in 1889. At Poulton, the layout was realigned involving over two miles of new route in 1896. The year 1903 saw the opening of a direct route from Kirkham to join the Lytham line just north of the then South Shore station. The track thence into Blackpool Central was quadrupled and a single track flyover provided to take up trains from the new line across the tracks from Talbot Road and Fleetwood to join the up fast line for Preston.

By the beginning of the present century, Blackpool Central had 14 platforms and Talbot Road 15, eight of them in a separate excursion station. There was a station at Waterloo Road on the 'new line' near the junction with the Lytham line. In 1916, this was equipped with platforms on both lines and South Shore station, a little way towards Lytham, was closed. Waterloo Road was renamed Blackpool South and Talbot Road became Blackpool North in 1932.

Rail-motors began operating from Talbot Road to Fleetwood in 1909, with additional halts provided at Poulton Curve and Burn Naze. Extra halts were also provided for a Blackpool Central – Lytham rail-motor service in 1913. Suspended during World War 1 this stopped again in 1939.

Across the narrow mouth of the Wyre from Fleetwood lies the village of Knott End. In 1863, local landowners promoted a company to construct a branch line from Garstang on the West Coast main line. In the spirit of the age they held out the prospect of the undertaking achieving main line status, and of the development of Knott End as a port to out-flank Fleetwood. Opening as far as Pilling was accomplished in December 1870, and for 15 months the line functioned with just one locomotive until the company went into receivership. Services resumed after three years in 1875.

The extension to Knott End was not achieved until 1908, and that was largely attributable to the sinking of salt mines at Preesall. In 1923, the London Midland & Scottish Railway absorbed the Garstang & Knott End Railway which by now had four locomotives, but withdrew passenger services in 1930. The line was cut back to Pilling in 1950, to Garstang Town in 1963, and disappeared completely two years after that. Knott End can today be reached by a small ferry from Fleetwood.

The year 1885 saw the inauguration of a standard gauge electric tramway along the Promenade between Pleasure Beach and Pleasant Street. Electrified initially on the conduit system, the line was converted to overhead in 1899 on being taken over by Blackpool Corporation. The network was then extended to include a number of street lines, around the town, and from 1903 enjoyed reciprocal

running powers with the neighbouring Lytham St Annes tramway undertaking.

At Gynn Square the Corporation tracks met, but did not join those of the Blackpool & Fleetwood Tramway which opened in 1898 from Talbot Road station to Fleetwood. The two termini were approached by street tracks, but between Gynn Square and Ash Street the line resembled a light railway, and in later years operated coal trains from the LMS exchange sidings near Ash Street to a depot at Thornton Gate. Blackpool Corporation purchased the Fleetwood route in 1920, subsequently connecting the line to its own system and integrating services.

In 1933, the Blackpool Corporation began a modernisation plan under which more than 100 streamlined cars were obtained from The English Electric Co Ltd. Although two branches were discarded, the remaining network which comprised the largely reserved track route from Starr Gate to Fleetwood, the street lines along Dickson Road to the North Station, along Lytham Road to Squires Gate Airport and the loop from Talbot Square to South Pier via Marton were retained as the most modern tramway operation in the British Isles. Hopes that this might extend along the entire coast to Lytham were ended when that borough closed its lines in 1937.

By 1961, a fashion swept the British Isles, though not the rest of Europe, suggesting that trams were old-fashioned. The last casualty of this attitude, the Glasgow network, was the final major mainland system outside Blackpool.

By 1961, Blackpool had just acquired some new rolling stock and work had begun on relaying the tracks in Lytham Road. Suddenly, Blackpool was no longer immune to the anti-tramway fever and the branch to Squires Gate Airport was closed that October reportedly because of the cost of track renewal. The Marton line closed a year later in the name of 'economy', and it was expected that the Dickson Road trams, for long accused of generating traffic congestion, would cease at the end of the 1963 season. When the announcement came it included winter closure of the 'Main Line' south of Cleveleys which henceforth was intended to operate in summer only. Problems with obtaining the necessary bus licence kept trams running between Cleveleys and Fleetwood. The next year, it was decided that the experiment had failed and so the Starr Gate – Fleetwood tramway service has operated throughout the year since 1964.

The 11-mile journey, particularly by a double-deck tram, is an experience unique in Europe. The line is regarded as an essential part of the Blackpool scene, and continues to carry a substantial residential traffic, particularly at the Fleetwood end.

Railway steamer services from Fleetwood to

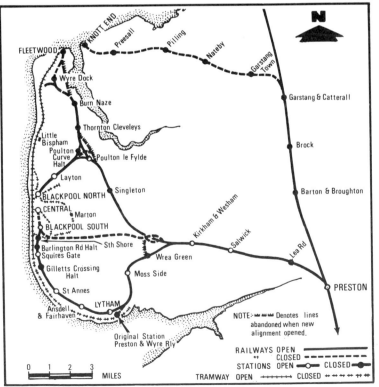

Above :

**Blackpool South in the 1950s,
with an express to Euston
headed by 'Jubilee' 4-6-0
No 45571** *South Africa.*
R. Hogan

N

FLEETWOOD
KNOTT END
Preesall
Pilling
Nateby
Garstang Town
Garstang & Catterall
Wyre Dock
Burn Naze
Brock
Thornton Cleveleys
Little
Bispham
Poulton
Curve
Halt
Poulton le Fylde
Layton
Singleton
BLACKPOOL NORTH
CENTRAL
Marton
BLACKPOOL SOUTH
Kirkham & Wesham
Barton & Broughton
Salwick
Sth Shore
Burlington Rd Halt
Squires Gate
Wrea Green
Gilletts Crossing
Halt
Moss Side
Lea Rd
St Annes
PRESTON
Ansdell
& Fairhaven
LYTHAM
NOTE: ⊶⊶ Denotes lines
abandoned when new
alignment opened.
Original Station
Preston & Wyre Rly

RAILWAYS OPEN ———
CLOSED – – –
STATIONS OPEN ○— CLOSED ●
TRAMWAY OPEN +—+—+ CLOSED +⊢+⊢+

0 1 2 3
MILES

122

Decline in the Fylde:

Top left:
In the last season of Blackpool Central's operations, a 'Britannia' 4-6-2 stands at Lytham St Annes with the summer Saturday 10.35am Glasgow Central–Blackpool Central on 11 July 1964. *W.S. Sellar*

Centre left:
Already under threat, Fleetwood station looks desolate on 1 August 1964. *J.A. Upton Woods*

Bottom left:
The stretch of line between Blackpool South and St Annes on the Sea was singled on 7 March 1982. Most of the second track remained in situ, except for a short length by the crossover at St Annes. On 30 November 1982, the 13.25 Blackpool South–Kirkham crosses from the 'wrong line' to the up line at the end of the singled section. *Richard G. Fox*

To return to the main line, the Beeching Report of 1963 recommended closure of the 'branch' from Poulton to Blackpool North. If Blackpool had to suffer any reduction in its railway facilities then the North Station, less convenient than Central and about to lose its tram connection, seemed the logical one to go. Early in 1964, BR made the surprising announcement that Blackpool North was to be retained at the expense of Central. South station was to become the terminus for trains from London, Manchester and Yorkshire, with North retaining a local service from Preston and East Lancashire. BR was therefore committed to maintaining two lines into Blackpool, neither of which penetrated the town centre. Central station closed in November 1964 and was sold to become a car-park and bingo hall. The justification for this astonishing move was apparently the value of the site. Some years later this was resold at a profit for more extensive redevelopment.

The direct line from Kirkham closed in 1966, but South remained the principal terminus until 1970 when traffic was transferred to North, leaving just a local service from Kirkham to Blackpool South. Though trains to Preston at peak-hours ceased some years later, along with Sunday services, and the line, nowadays single track beyond St Annes, sees lengthy gaps between trains. In 1974, Blackpool North station was reconstructed on the site of the former excursion platforms. The erstwhile main station became a supermarket, and the trains were banished that much further from the sea-front and town centre.

Fleetwood station went the same way as Blackpool Central in 1966 when the line was cut back to Wyre Dock. Like Blackpool South, there were assurances that this terminus would be suitably

Ireland ended in 1928 when the LMS elected to concentrate its Irish Sea operations on Heysham. However, the Isle of Man Steam Packet Company continued its summer service. According to *Bradshaw*, the luxurious geared turbine steamer *Lady of Mann* (23 knots) 'or other steamer will take the first morning sailing from Fleetwood and the afternoon sailing from Douglas each weekday'. Unfortunately, the landing stage adjacent to Fleetwood station was found unsuitable for use after 1961. A new berth was opened in 1971 and a summer service resumed of up to five sailings a week, latterly much restricted following the reduction in the fleet forced by competition from Sealink's Isle of Man route operating out of Heysham.

service to Belfast and Dublin, all traffic for which is transported by road.

Ever since electrification from Crewe to Glasgow was announced in 1970, the Manchester to Blackpool line has been regarded as a priority for extension of the overhead wires. Not only would it improve the service operating over this important commuter and holiday route, but the locomotive changes at Preston which now frustrate Manchester to Scotland and London to Blackpool workings would be eliminated, too.

A possibility discussed, but apparently rejected by Blackpool Corporation, would involve extending the tramway over railway tracks from Squires Gate to St Annes at which BR's operations would then terminate. Unless St Annes were to be included in the BR electrification plans and equipped with through trains to Preston, the trams might as well run all the way to Kirkham. Applying the same logic, the only way now to restore a service into Fleetwood would be to connect the surviving goods line to the tramway north of Rossall and run trams from Poulton to Fleetwood. This may seem like science fiction to anyone who has not witnessed tramway/light railway development in continental Europe.

Although a tremendous proportion of the day-trip/holiday traffic has been lost (or given away) to road transport, what remains is augmented by a considerable volume of conference and commuter traffic. The passengers naturally wish to travel to different parts of the Fylde peninsula. BR has abandoned its Central terminus in Blackpool, completely withdrawn from North Fylde and left a branch line, now seemingly regarded as an embarrassment, to serve the south. The resulting situation is the worst of all worlds and need not have happened if a co-ordinated public transport system had been in existence 20 years ago. It would be fitting if the Blackpool Tramways, a pioneer system in the past, could be developed to reconnect Fleetwod and Lytham St Annes to the main line network.

Above:
The site of Blackpool Central Station, as seen from the Tower in August 1971.   *R.E. Ruffell*

Below:
The rebuilt Blackpool North station, viewed on 31 May 1980. The diesel railcar formation waits as the Saturday 19.25 for Colne, and the stock of a Euston train is on the right.   *Brian Morrison*

upgraded. It was renamed Fleetwood and saw a service to Poulton, with the occasional train venturing as far as Kirkham, until closure in 1970. The line continues to serve a chemical works at Burn Naze and Fleetwood power station. This is all that remains of a line which once carried boat trains, commuters and extensive fish traffic. Former railway land is used for a P & O/B & I line container

Beeching – 20 years on

John Booth

THE BEATLES and Beeching were in the news during 1963. Twenty years later, the first-named were back in the hit parade, but what about Beeching? He was anything but a hit in 1963 but, like the famous four, an echo could be found 20 years later. Beeching had come to the fore in 1961 as a result of the Stedeford Committee of 1960, one of the periodical Governmental investigations into British Railways, and by 1981 they were at it again: the Serpell Committee was sieving through the evidence once more and reported in 1983. Almost a

Left:
With cigar in hand, Dr Beeching looks at the London Design Centre's *The New Face of British Railways* **exhibition which he opened on 4 January 1965.** *Council of Industrial Design*

generation later, what effect did the Beeching prescription have on the patient?

Two things are immediately worth saying. The process of apparently squaring the books by cutting the railway network was not new. Of the Regions, only the Eastern had pursued a concerted policy of rationalisation, but by 1961/62 it was clear that drastic measures were needed. Someone at the top had to enshrine rationalisation as a systemwide policy. The second aspect of Beeching is that the public relations handling of the presentation of the famous report – *The Reshaping of British Railways*, HMSO April 1963 – was maladroit. The closures got all the attention. By including an alphabetical list of stations 'to be closed' – taking up 20 pages of the Report out of 148 – every newspaper promptly repeated the catalogue. The essentially negative aspects of what was seen in the Report as only one part of a process of reshaping the business got the headlines. Beeching was the axe-man. Even more remarkably, I have been told that it had been intended to publish the closures *first*, then follow up the death list with an outline for development. This was logical in the sense that the Report was adamant that the 'lumber' should be cleared out first – 'it is obvious that a high proportion of stopping passenger train services ought to be discontinued as soon as possible'. That was one of the strongest statements in the Report. However, it is difficult to believe that the reshaping process would have made any headway if the closures had been promulgated first. 'Clearing out the lumber' was symptomatic of the age. It was unthinkable to Beeching that apparently obvious facts should not be acted upon. The smart newspapers of the period were full of phrases such as taking a 'long, cool look'. Beeching was the sort of man who fitted in well with Anthony Sampson's *Anatomy of Britain* (published 1962). To

The negative face of the Beeching era:

Above:
The Banff–Tillynaught branch was singled out for exceptional stricture: the 7.50pm from Banff waits unprofitably behind BR '2' 2-6-0 No 78045 on 5 July 1963. *W.G. Sumner*

Sampson, 'His arrival in British Railways has within a year already produced a new situation. . . he . . . has brought a whole new vocabulary. . .' Well, yes. Talking first and doing afterwards were all-important. Certainly, no one had attempted an over-view of BR since nationalisation. By 1962, the system's finances were deteriorating fast. BR's operating ratio (the percentage of working expenses to receipts) soared from 109 in 1959 to 123 in 1962. Two Regions, the Western and London Midland, were in deep trouble. The Beeching Report was intelligent enough to see that there was a whole series of interlinked problems and that 'neither modernisation nor more economical working could make the railways viable in their existing form, and that a reshaping of the whole pattern of business would be necessary as well'.

The recasting of the 'whole pattern of business' is where the Beeching approach began to show its flaws – in hindsight. Curiously enough, despite the extensive surveys of traffic in 1961, and the production of the famous maps, some of the general conclusions drawn about the operation of the railway network were incomplete. The maps certainly demonstrated the characteristics of a national railway network serving a variety of thinly and thickly populated areas. 'One half of the system earns far less than sufficient to cover the cost of providing the route to permit the movement. . . By contrast, the other half of the system has earnings which cover its route costs more than six times'. That was as far as it went. In the next paragraph in the Report's review of the network was the statement that although the contributory value of traffics on lightly loaded lines was not at that stage being considered in the Report, the fact was that 'most of the traffics fed to the rest of the sytem are of the less favourable kinds.' However, it is the subsequent exercise in which the contributory revenue is assessed that is the least convincing. A number of plums were picked out – such as the Banff-Tillynaught branch with 37,400 train miles annually generating £800 revenue – and the assumption was that each service could be taken in isolation. Nowhere in the Report is there any indication that its authors had attempted to understand *how* a railway network worked, in terms of inter-related services using the same track and stations. By identifying that there was a core of 12,800 route-miles out of a total of 17,830 in 1961 which *was* redeemable, it was assumed that the process of contraction would inevitably result in greatly reduced system costs. As the greatest losses were in fact being made on the heaviest worked sections, the belief that lopping off the branches would reduce the deficit significantly was misplaced. Perhaps it was not so evident at the time when many rural railways were self-evidently a profligate waste of resources. Would it not have been better to cut out the worst and aim to work the rest more efficiently?

The genuinely disinterested approach of the Beeching investigators was not in doubt in much of their Report, but critical though they were of traditional railwaymen, at least one shibboleth was taken on board. Beeching was wont to say, 'there is no more frequent or sadder testimonial than "we have always done it this way" '. But the Reshaping Report, at this point well into its stride, came out with: 'These points (decreased fares, higher fares, railbuses for ordinary trains, reduced services, or less stations) have been mentioned' (in fact, rebutted)'in order to dispose of any idea that stopping train services could be preserved. . . if only some ingenuity were shown by railway operators. This really is not so. . .'

In fact, Beeching was wrong. The Norwich Division of the Eastern Region showed that in Norfolk the basic railway with pay-train operations could go most of the way to recovering the direct costs of movement. Unhappily, the contemporary rationalisation of the freight and parcels business meant that the passenger revenue had to carry the whole of the operating costs out-country. The result was that some of Norfolk's basic railway had a brief reprieve indeed. A less dogmatic approach in the Beeching Report might have elicited the support of local authorities towards financing the upkeep of their lines. By the time a more intelligent attitude prevailed at the top, people had voted with their feet. The Beeching Report's obsession with cutting out mileage inevitably frightened off people from rural railways. Good traffic followed bad.

The principle of breaking-down the railway network into trains that paid their way and those that didn't led to an impossible quest. Friends of mine on BR at the time scrutinised drivers' tickets and other evidence by the ton in the effort to isolate the cost of running a train. With the BR passenger network underwritten by national and local Government to the tune of £810m in 1981, or 44% of passenger traffic income, the search for the profitable train has seemed a chimera. But *The Reshaping of British Railways* Report talked in terms of eliminating *much* ('though not necessarily all' – they hastily qualified themselves!) of BR's deficit by 1970. Given that Beeching was out of the Chairmanship by early 1965 and that some of the

vigour of the approach went also, it is sobering to note that although the overall loss declined from £182.6m in 1962 to £123m in 1964, it was back to £153m by 1967. Why didn't the results look better?

The reason was that in the haste to divest the railways of its 'uneconomic' network, accompanied by the inevitable storm that was raised, many of the commercial decisions made were wrong. The drive to get the bulk oil and general trainload traffic was right, as was (some) of the insistence on the rationalisation of facilities and train working. But when it came to developing services, the Beeching approach was on less sure ground.

In the Report there was comment to the effect that the proposals put forward were 'restrainedly speculative' as far as new developments were concerned. In the case of InterCity traffic, the analysis concluded that receipts for fast and semi-fast inter-city trains had been 'stable and may be expected to remain so but had not kept pace with rising costs'. Rural services had been written off as revenue-earners, as were the networks serving London and other metropolitan centres. Wagonload freight and freight sundries were also written off – block trains were the answer. The Doctor's panacea was the development of a new countrywide Liner Train (=Freightliner) integrated system which would be in full operation by 1970. It would handle the merchandise traffic abstracted from existing wagonload services, the profitable part of the sundries business, parcels movements and a proportion of roadborne traffic otherwise denied to rail. Only Liner Trains would provide a sizeable contribution to the system costs.

In effect, everything was staked on the Liner Trains, although an as yet untried system, despite the fact that there was no evidence that the service would be attractive to customers. As Gerard Fiennes has related in *I tried to run a railway* (pub Ian Allan Ltd, revised ed 1973), by late 1963 'Liner Trains were in the inevitable second stage. . . the rats of doubt were gnawing at the edges'. The container revolution was beginning to take place, but the impetus was from the deepsea shipping lines and they were to call the tune. Meanwhile, the wagonload business was fast being rationalised under the National Freight Train Plan of the mid-1960s. Sure, the wagon fleet was being made much more efficient, but at the cost of a second-class service and without any investment in new vehicles. Before long, the 1968 Transport Act took the initiative away from the BRB and placed it with the new National Freight Corporation. With a change

Left:
Freight service salvation, as seen by Beeching. A prototype Liner train wagon and containers go on show in 1964. *BR*

127

of Government, that authority steadily became road-minded. It would be 1973 before the BRB put up the air-braked freight train network – Speedlink. By then it was almost too late. Road freight, benefiting from the creation of the motorway network and a rapid improvement in vehicle technology, had pinched most of the best traffic.

In short, the promise of dynamic management developing those traffic flows most suited to rail was not realised. In Gerard Fiennes' view 'the Central Direction (BRB) had been trying to manage instead of giving itself time to think'.

The development of freight train block working and the merry-go-round operations for power station coal was successfully achieved, but the business potential was finite, although in time the volume of traffic was better than foreseen by Beeching. So the main emphasis could only be on InterCity. Beeching's successor as the Chairman of the BRB, Stanley Raymond, deserves much of the credit in this case for central direction that worked. He was helped by the completion of the London Midland Region's main line electrification from Euston to Manchester and Liverpool, and by the Eastern Region's hard work in developing the East Coast main line diesel worked InterCity services, owing much to the 'Deltics'. Also the Mark 2 coaches, then coming into service, were a thoroughly good product, capable of sustained 100mph running.

Beeching, however, had an unusual viewpoint on what came to be the InterCity 'product'. Like the apocryphal Irish railway which ushered passengers into each compartment of a coach until it was full and then, and only then, let the train leave as it was loaded, Beeching believed in relatively few, heavily loaded trains on principal routes. He did not subscribe to the Fiennes/Raymond principle of regular interval light, fast trains. The Anglo-Scottish day trains were viewed as a busted flush. Hence, the 1964 Beeching Part 2, *The Development of the Major Railway Trunk Routes,* saw no difficulty in truncating the principal East Coast trains by relegating the Newcastle-Edinburgh main line to secondary status. In time, the East Coast Anglo-Scottish day trains, cheerfully ignoring the diktat of little or nothing north of Newcastle, were to be among BR's principal money-spinners.

Similarly, *Trunk Routes* was ready to write off the Reading-Westbury-Taunton and Salisbury-Exeter

main lines as secondary routes. It took a lot of effort to persuade West Country opinion that BR wanted traffic from the west at all. Both routes were starved of investment until a crash programme of improvements on the Berks and Hants route from the late 1970s. Despite being a good revenue earner, the Salisbury-Exeter line is still hampered by the rationalisation programme of the mid-1960s, although the post-Serpell track mileage reduction proposals look like reducing Castle Cary-Taunton to similar standards.

More surprisingly perhaps, the Beeching viewpoint saw the InterCity network as principally serving the needs of businessmen. The emphasis was on catering for the expense account briefcase-carrier rather than the Jimmy Saville Railcard-bearing holdall-carrier of the 1980s. The mass-travel potential of the InterCity network was not foreseen. The 1963 Report saw the main challenge being posed by the private car and internal air services, revealing its pre-occupation with the well-heeled traveller, rather than with those not owning cars. This approach naturally downgraded the role of the cross-country routes which were to wait until the 1970s before diesel multiple units were taken off in favour of loco-hauled trains running on more attractive schedules.

But of course all this is hindsight. By posing the threat of closure for 5,000 route miles of passenger service, and suggesting that social benefit costing might be adopted for suburban services in London and elsewhere, came the basis of the grant-aided network of today. The Beeching era made mistakes, and the cost savings so promisingly offered in the prospectus were never fully realised. The commercial judgements were not soundly based and it was left to practical railwaymen to evolve the patterns of service over the ensuing decade. Labour relations were proccupied with redundancies until the Penzance agreement of 1968 sought to produce a better deal for railwaymen. The high cost of operating the basic core of the system was only subjected to cliff-hanging decision-making in the early 1980s. Of course, it could have been done better, without much of the trauma of the 1963-68 period, but it would have demanded superhuman standards from management. Better to reflect, it would seem, that BR has survived the harsh economic environment of the last few years better than anyone would have dared hope.